Sacred Moments, Holy Days

SACRED MOMENTS, HOLY DAYS

Stories of Life, Service, and Grace

Michael Maiello

SHEED & WARD

Franklin, Wisconsin

As an apostolate of the Priests of the Sacred Heart, a Catholic religious congregation, the mission of Sheed & Ward is to publish books of contemporary impact and enduring merit in Catholic Christian thought and action. The books published, however, reflect the opinions of their authors and are not meant to represent the official position of the Priests of the Sacred Heart.

2001

Sheed & Ward
7373 South Lovers Lane Road
Franklin, Wisconsin 53132
1-800-266-5564

Copyright © 2001 by Michael Maiello

All rights reserved. No part of this book may be reproduced, stored in a retrieval system, or transmitted in any form or by any means—electronic, mechanical, photocopying, recording, or otherwise—without the written permission of Sheed & Ward.

Disclaimer: The identities of the people referred to in this book have been carefully disguised in accordance with professional standards of confidentiality and in keeping with their rights to privileged communication with the author.

Scripture quotations are from the New Revised Standard Version of the Bible, copyright 1989 by the Division of Christian Education of the National Council of the Churches of Christ in the USA. Used by permission. All rights reserved.

Cover and interior design: GrafixStudio, Inc.
Cover photos provided by Cleo Photography, the Evansville Mission, and Scott Wannemuehler.

Library of Congress Cataloging-in-Publication Data
Maiello, Michael.
    Sacred moments, holy days : stories of life, service, and grace / Michael Maiello.
      p. cm.
    Includes bibliographical references.
    ISBN 1-58051-097-3 (alk. paper)
  1. Catholic Church—United States—Charities. 2. Church and social problems—Catholic Church. 3. Church and social problems—United States. I. Title.
BX2347 .M35 2001
267'.18273—dc21   00-053339

1 2 3 4 5 / 04 03 02 01

Dedication

With deepest gratitude
to my colleagues and family

Contents

Acknowledgments *viii*

Preface *ix*

Prologue: Beginnings and Arrivals *xi*

Part One: Secret People *1*

Part Two: Streets and Horizons *37*

Part Three: The Recesses of the North *81*

Epilogue: Endtime and Renewal *117*

Notes *120*

Acknowledgments

This book could not have been written without the friendship and support of Irene Seraffin, Patricia Matson, Bro. Thomas Grady, O.S.F., Msgr. Mark Giordani, Karen Lordi, Virginia Grossi, Lucy Severini, Sr. Dorothy Sheahan, S.C., and Rev. Norman O'Connor, C.P.S. I am deeply grateful for their more than generous spirit.

Kass Dotterweich deserves special recognition for her proficient editing and valuable advice.

Finally, I must acknowledge the encouragement I received from my parents, Michael and Ida, and from Mark, Jennifer, and Michael Damian Maiello. Each of them, in their own way, helped bring this book to fruition.

Preface

At the time of this writing, I have completed twenty-four years of service as a social worker, attorney, and administrator at Catholic Charities. I began in the Diocese of Brooklyn, New York, and then spent twelve years in the Diocese of Paterson, New Jersey. In its organizational literature, Catholic Charities agencies often dazzle people with extensive listings of the services they provide and their plans to expand its services to meet new needs. This information, as valid and useful as it is, does not convey a real sense of the work being done, person to person, day after day, by Charities' staff. It fails to communicate the holy encounters that permeate this work and speak to the hearts of those involved.

In this book I have attempted to describe some of the encounters and experiences I have had with adults, children, and families in distress. Each has assumed a special place in my memory and faith. Except for a few, all occurred during my more recent ministry in Paterson. I have also included reflections on personal and other professional experiences that took place during that time; these are offered as relevant to the book's theme. Events related herein that are not from Paterson are specifically identified as such.

People who serve others for a meaningful period of time are exposed to an unavoidable, fundamental truth: the essential vulnerability of us all. Christ's life, from birth to death and resurrection, proclaims that this fragility need not defeat us. He teaches that every one of us, prodigals all, are cherished for our own sakes and are always limitlessly loved by God. We can flee from this love, insisting it does not exist and maintaining our egos as best we can in a universe so immense our being appears of no import, or we can accept it, as freely and unconditionally available, without surcease. This is a most wondrous love to accept. It liberates and empowers us to be family whether, at any given moment, we are the brother asking for help or the sister called to give it.

Prologue

~

Beginnings and Arrivals

When I graduated from St. John's University School of Law in 1973 and was admitted to the New York State Bar in 1974, I should have been a happy person, but I was not. I had become an attorney with the express purpose of working for Legal Aid or Legal Services and had failed to find employment with either organization. The jobs I had been offered with private firms and businesses left me cold. I was becoming increasingly impatient and alarmed and wasn't at all sure what to do.

Every Sunday I scoured the employment pages of the *New York Times* looking for promising jobs. There never seemed to be work for a lawyer who wanted to help the poor, but always a ceaseless abundance of openings in real estate and matrimonial firms and, of course, collection agencies. The idea of serving others, which had been nurtured in me during my undergraduate, pseudo-revolutionary, anti-war, anti-poverty days, seemed destined to reduce me to poverty despite my education.

Finally, out of desperation, I answered an ad for the position of caseworker at a well-established, Catholic foster-care agency in Brooklyn. The job entailed visiting twenty to thirty foster homes a month to ensure that the children placed in each home were being properly cared for and that, when appropriate, social workers were properly preparing the children's legal parents for their offsprings' return. Sometimes it meant planning for the adoption of children whose parents had clearly abandoned them. To my surprise, I got the job. As far as I know, I have been the only licensed attorney, foster-care caseworker in New York. I enjoyed the work immensely, despite having to explain why I wasn't practicing law to far too many people.

It was a deep expression of my parents' love to support this decision to become a caseworker, even though it seemed I was wasting my legal education. As I mentioned, however, I had given ample warning, while I was a student, of the path I would choose. During college I worked in a summer program for underprivileged children sponsored by St. John's University. I participated in demonstrations, on campus and in Manhattan, against the war in Vietnam, and I was active in developing support in the university for Cesar Chavez and the United Farm Workers, helping to organize the picketing of supermarkets selling produce from non-union growers. For years my mother honored my endeavors by buying only UFW-approved grapes and lettuce for the family. During those years, I wanted to be of some use to people and attempted to set the course of my life toward that end, rather than trying to accumulate influence and money.

The proverbial door opened for me at the end of 1975, when I was hired as the Assistant Director of Legal Affairs for Brooklyn Catholic Charities. The title was less lofty than it might imply. There were only two attorneys for legal affairs, the woman who was my director and myself. It was nice of her to make me an assistant director, and I will always be thankful to her for the healing effect the title had on my parents. My having a business card, an actual title, and an office of my own made them feel I had avoided maladjustment.

I was grateful finally to be practicing law in an organization dedicated to helping people. That this organization was part of the Church was an added bonus because, following high school, prayer, meditation, and retreats had become increasingly important to me. In college I majored in philosophy and minored in theology. I read Dorothy Day, Thomas Merton, Dietrich Bonhoeffer, Simone Weil, and other teachers of spirituality and Christian activism whenever I could throughout law school. To work for the Church was a blessing. To work for that part of the Church specifically created to serve the needy was to be doubly blessed.

My responsibilities included resolving contractual problems with the various merchants and landlords we dealt with, and drafting comments on proposed state and federal legislation that might affect the poor or the agency. Best of all, I gave legal advice to social workers and their clients on matters ranging from landlord-tenant, public-assistance, disability, and social security issues to matrimonial and support problems. When I worked with clients, I remember their surprise at the amount of time and attention they were given; it was as if being poor meant, by definition, that they were not worthy of such care.

After five years I was offered and accepted the position of Assistant to the Executive Director. This was my entrée into administration and it was an important learning experience for me. Brooklyn Catholic Charities provided every social service imaginable at that time, from emergency assistance to people in crisis to long-term housing for the elderly and disabled. Its staff numbered over fifteen hundred, and its budget was in the millions and growing. As a member of the organization's administrative staff, I inevitably saw enough to form strong opinions about the agency's operation: the way its services were offered and delivered; its sense of identity and mission and how these were conveyed to staff; what was considered critical and what was not.

I have no doubt that the services provided by Brooklyn Catholic Charities were superior to those being offered by government programs in New York City, be they municipal, state, or federal. The agency had a sense of professionalism that extended to its entire staff, whatever their responsibilities. It was a place I was proud to work in because I knew that a genuine effort was being made to create and maintain quality programs. However, as with most service-oriented charitable organizations, there was a struggle between mission and margin.

During my time in Brooklyn, I voiced concern about the growing gap between administrators and the people their programs served and the increasing emphasis being put on the bottom line. I promised myself that if I ever became an executive director of Catholic Charities, wherever that might be, I would work hard to make the agency as Christian as possible in its operation, by putting the concerns of the poor above all else.

In 1986 I was given the opportunity to attempt this. That year I was appointed Diocesan Director of Catholic Charities in Paterson, New Jersey—a small diocese consisting of three counties in the northern part of the state. Leaving Brooklyn to go there was initially shocking; everything was reduced in dimension by comparison. The size of the cities in the diocese—Paterson and Passaic—the agency and its staff, and even my office were like nothing I had previously experienced. Paterson is noted as the birthplace of Lou Costello (of Abbott and Costello comedic fame) and of the beat poet Alan Ginsberg, whose poem "Howl" has become a classic. I could understand what drove him to howling: the city is economically depressed, with a shortage of jobs and housing. There was, and still is, no lack of drug addiction, alcoholism, homelessness, and violence. AIDS became epidemic. It is a place where people need to have Catholic Charities.

During the next twelve years I tried to realize goals that were, for me, the reasons for being in Paterson. I wanted to expand services to meet the evident needs and problems of people in the diocese and make sure that all of the agency's resources were used to that end. All administrators, including myself, were to be involved in some manner of direct service so that we could experience the helping mission of the agency. I sought a working environment in which no one lorded power over anyone else but, rather, where we respected one another as professional colleagues and personally cared for one another as family. Finally, and of greatest import, our family was to include those we served, who were never to be treated or regarded as less than ourselves.

That these goals were attained had much less to do with anything I did than with the dedication and spirituality of the staff I worked with. Their efforts made it possible for me to evoke the experiences and reflections that are the substance of this book. So, beginning in Brooklyn, I arrived in Paterson, a place I grew to love and for years thought I would never leave. In both places I met those I call secret people: the men, women, and children living on the margin of our society, whom most of us never see. I saw neglect and suffering in abundance. Sometimes I sensed the "recesses of the North," majestic as in Psalm 48, where God abides and we are never turned away. Recesses, I came to see, that are within us all.

Part One

Secret People

Daniel was what people call a "bit slow upstairs." He lived alone on Atlantic Avenue in Brooklyn, seldom venturing more than a few blocks from home. This may have been because he didn't want to get lost—or because he simply never wanted to go farther, I'm not certain. I do know that being fifty years old or so, Daniel could recite much of the history of where he had lived for the past thirty years. He knew all of the businesses and shops, the owners, their families, who had moved away, who had taken their place, people's proclivities, who was friendly, who was not.

I met Daniel because his new landlord had decided to take advantage of his condition and was attempting to evict him for nonpayment of rent. Daniel had fallen two months behind, and his landlord, by voiding the remainder of the existing lease, could immediately increase the rent for Daniel's apartment. Rooms are always at a premium in Brooklyn, and finding another tenant would be no problem. That the eviction would violate the pattern of Daniel's life, which gave him the security he needed to live well, also appeared to be no problem for the landlord.

At that time, I was a young attorney practicing poverty law, among other duties, at Brooklyn Catholic Charities. I had already seen enough, however, to know that helping Daniel would not be easy.

Daniel was terrified by the eviction notice. He had been raised by an aunt, who had long ago died, and felt secure only when in his little enclave. He wasn't at all sure he could function if he had to leave his apartment. As I listened to him and got to know him, I wasn't sure he could either. He had difficulty finding my office, and I needed to go over the return directions with him in detail, which included taking a bus.

My new client worked as a floor waxer for a small company and, although he was paid only slightly more than the minimum wage, he earned enough money to make his rent and provide for his other necessities. This was solely because his current rent was so low. The problem was that Daniel liked to buy things and, too often, gave in to this temptation when he got paid. He liked fancy shoes and had several pairs, and he bought many religious medallions, which he wore for protection and as reminders to pray. He loved music and unhesitatingly purchased albums (cassettes were not yet on the market). He enjoyed Chinese and Italian food and had it delivered to his apartment. He was, God bless him, savoring life as best he could.

I answered the eviction notice with a request for a hearing in Landlord-Tenant Court that, by law, had to be honored. This meant that Daniel was safe, at least for the next five weeks, until the date of the hearing. Landlord-Tenant Court is traditionally a place of expeditious adjudication: the rent due has been paid or not. There is usually little precedence or patience for extenuating circumstances. The court calendar is always backed up, and quick decisions in favor of landlords, especially in nonpayment matters, are the rule. To help Dan, I would have to make a big deal out of this case—in essence, force the hearing examiner to stop, take time, and give consideration to the special circumstances involved.

An agency social worker, Karen, was assigned to Daniel, and together we began working to keep him at home. Karen is a great person and exceptional social worker who, from the start, was determined that Daniel wasn't going anywhere. He liked her immediately, as did I, and both of us were immensely relieved to have her help. It was Karen who designed a contingency plan should the worst occur. This plan included putting Daniel's belongings in storage, finding another apartment he could afford and move in to, regardless of location, and contacting, as a last resort, a men's shelter that Daniel could use if necessary. This done, the three of us worked to assure that none of it would happen.

Our immediate task was to place Daniel on a total emergency budget. Absolutely every dollar he could save before the hearing had to be put aside toward the sum he owed in back rent. This would amount to over three months' worth, since his landlord would not accept a cent prior to the court date (he knew that to do so would obviate his request for eviction). Every week Daniel cashed his paycheck, gave his earnings to Karen, and received back just enough to cover his necessities. Karen held the remainder in escrow, locked away safely at the agency. In this way, Daniel saved an amount equaling slightly more than two months' rent. Catholic Charities was able to give him the difference he owed, plus an additional full month's rent that the landlord could use as future security.

The hearing was held on a gorgeous morning of sunlight and breeze, the kind of day that often deceives me into believing good things are about to happen. Karen, Daniel, and I were early; Daniel in shirt and tie, very excited, hopeful and frightened at the same time. The landlord, as plaintiff, began by stating his position, giving the facts tersely, with the ease of someone who has done this many times before. He knew the law and was confident about the forthcoming decision.

Karen opened our case by describing Daniel's problems and his success in overcoming them. She explained that forcing Daniel to leave his apartment and neighborhood would certainly prevent him from continuing the independent life he had tried so hard to create. He would not be able to find his way to work and would not be able to find a new job as amenable as the one he had. He would soon become a public charge despite his willingness to work. "All of this," Karen said, "because he was late paying two months' rent."

I then presented our checks to the court and promised that Catholic Charities would continue to work with Daniel to make sure he paid his rent on time. I also submitted a letter from Daniel's employer that praised him as a conscientious worker whose loss would be felt should he not be able to keep his job.

I then asked Daniel to describe to the hearing examiner his feelings about what was happening. In response, Daniel was open about his fear of moving, about having to be in a new place he didn't know, and about losing the job he liked so much. He also talked about the many friends he had where he lived and how he didn't want to leave them. Finally, he apologized to the hearing examiner and to his landlord for falling behind in his rent and swore he would never do it again.

Sensing that the examiner was intrigued and perplexed, we willing complied when he asked us to leave the room for a few minutes while he thought things through. While we waited, Daniel's landlord remained adamant and began to get angry, Daniel continued to expect good news, Karen looked bravely secure, and I just tried my best to appear minimally resolute. When we were called back into the courtroom, the examiner asked Karen and me to assure him Catholic Charities would, indeed, help Daniel make all future rent payments on time, as I had promised—and I knew that we had won. We gave our assurance, and the examiner denied the petition for eviction.

Before dismissing us, the examiner gave Daniel a little lecture on the importance of making timely payments; he also gave a longer lecture to Daniel's landlord about the futility of taking retribution on his tenant—little things like shutting off his water or not providing heat. Should that happen, the examiner said, he would personally order Daniel's rent withheld until the matter was corrected and would go further by levying whatever fines he deemed appropriate.

Walking out into the bright sunlight that morning, I thought that the three years I had labored in law school were almost worth it. A Hungarian tenant, a Polish-American Jewish social worker, an Italian-American attorney, and an African-American hearing examiner had shown that it was still possible to protect a vulnerable person. Things were not completely in favor of the "haves."

Full of triumph and righteousness, I asked Daniel and Karen to an early lunch. Karen, however, had to see another client and couldn't join us. After she gave Daniel a long kiss on the cheek, which he returned with gratitude, we watched her go off, once more, to work.

Daniel and I then went to a deli I knew on Boerum Avenue to celebrate. I remember ordering pastrami on rye with extra mustard and a large root beer. Daniel, having listened to me very carefully, ordered the same. After the sandwiches, and content with victory and food, Daniel said, out of nowhere, "You know, Mike, even though I have some friends, I think I'm the kind of guy who's easy to forget. I think, sometimes, I'm kind of a secret person." Before I could react with a torrent of palliative words meant to make him feel better about himself, he added, "and so are you."

Stopped in my tracks, I saw that Daniel was quite at ease with this and was sure I was, too, so evident was its truth to him. I suggested we have dessert and we both had apple pie á la mode with butter pecan ice cream and steaming hot coffee. I began to feel at peace with the idea of being forgotten and, for a moment, Daniel and I were happy being secret in the world.

You are in your late fifties, too old to use the drugs the young ones mix with their liquor. So when you've bummed money enough, you drink belts of wine and whiskey. It makes everything nice these early winter evenings; makes you warm, or at least it helps you forget you're cold.

You find a place in the dead brush and the low trees near the highway, where you can't be seen, and you drink and smoke Camels, the real ones, not the lights with filters, and you remember better times, places you've lived, and people you've loved, now long gone. You cry a little to yourself and thank God that you've got the wine and the whiskey and the cigarettes—and that it's not all that cold tonight. You drink, steadily, with purpose and rhythm, smoking in rhythm with the drinking. Slowly, you stop thinking of the past and forget any future that might be and start feeling peaceful and, for a while, just right. You keep drinking until the drink is gone and all you have are the Camels, and you smoke while trains go by on which no one can see you and you keep smoking until the sickness comes like you knew it would.

The sickness means you can't close your eyes or lie down because your brain won't permit it. Your mind rejects what your eyes show it, and you have to sit up and try to lie down and sit up again for hours, your chin on your knees, eyes wide open to prevent what you see from whirring away. What's left of your stomach wants to leave you and you try to let it, forcing two or three fingers as far down your throat as you can, retching on the leaves and weeds three times, then a fourth, until your stomach agrees to remain with you and most of the alcohol is gone, except for what is left in your blood to let you sleep black sleep, without nightmares you can remember.

You sleep until late morning, maybe ten o'clock, when you can stand without reeling, then you sleep some more until it's afternoon and you can walk again to Brooklyn Heights, where there are places you can beg change for cigarettes and wine. You won't be able to beg enough for the whiskey, too, unless you have great luck.

The last thing you want is for anyone to preach to you or try to save you. The person people want to save was lost years ago, for reasons it's no one's business to know but you—for you to remember or forget as you see fit.

There's a longing in your stomach and a calling in your mind for wine, and you will give them both what they want as soon as you can, after eating soup and a sandwich at the mission. You know real winter is coming and if you haven't the strength or desire to leave Brooklyn, you will begin what you call "wintering," a word you like. It almost brings romance to a man's life on the bum, which for days and nights in the cold is a constant search for comfort; a routine of begging, drinking, avoiding the police, eating at the mission, finding places out of the weather to rest—hidden places that are safe—using the overnight shelters only when you must because they don't allow booze.

You tell me all this because for a few minutes you want to talk to someone about yourself; then you stop, completely. You take what you need from the clothes we have—a sweater, socks, and a ski cap—and when you leave I barely hear you mutter, "Everyone can go to hell as far as I'm concerned."

Our janitor had a practice of breaking old, inedible bread and leaving it for the pigeons and sparrows that choose to nest in Brooklyn. One morning, after a night of sporadic rain, I saw an elderly man picking up pieces of thoroughly soaked bread and eating them. He moved methodically from puddle to puddle, trying to make sure he didn't miss a crumb. He was concentrating so hard that I startled him with the offer of some real food if he would just, please, come with me. Instead of cursing me or ignoring me, as I half expected, he grasped my wrist. His whole body seemed to be shaking, and I had to help him into an office where one of our staff began working to keep him alive and safe. He told me he was living on the streets and was contemplating suicide, having lost all sense of presence in the world. He asked for rest and a priest to talk to, and was provided both, after a hot meal. Later, we settled him in a homeless shelter where he will be fed and receive counseling.

This man remains in my memory, rending my heart whenever he comes to mind. For me, he has become a salient example of the lostness of us all, and of our need for one another during times of crisis. I have known too many people who have taken their lives, either by overdosing or by more immediate means. I can only speculate whether they would still have done so had they waited a day or another week or two. They might have found discarded bread commending them to others who could have helped them change their minds. They might have found bread enough to believe they were not alone. No one will ever know. We may someday find that sparrows were treated more kindly than they were.

Arturo was blind and approaching seventy. Unabashed, he came to us seeking a wife to ameliorate his loneliness and to "bring the caring that only a woman can" to the last days of his life. He was a very religious, very trusting man who, having presented us with his problem, was able to completely relax, fully expecting us to solve it. Perhaps he sensed that we were drawn to him, as much for his bravado as for his romanticism. Despite the obvious odds against finding the woman Arturo was confidently waiting to wed, the staff felt they had to do something.

We utilized two discreet means of discovery. First, we integrated Arturo, as best we could, into the agency's senior citizen activities, hoping, in time, that he might meet someone compatible. Concurrently, we asked Arturo's pastor if there might be a promising candidate in his parish, and Monsignor Torrelli was more than cooperative. In his next Sunday homily, he used Arturo's plight as an example of human need that could be addressed, say, by volunteers willing to help with housecleaning, food shopping, and cooking chores. Monsignor and I were both astounded when, within a week, two women asked to meet our bachelor, each interested in exploring a much more meaningful relationship.

Blind for forty-one years, Arturo was nonetheless capable of finding his own way. He moved slowly but safely, with the confidence and authority his age commanded. Without hesitation, he began dating Teresa, one of the women who had expressed interest. In a matter of a few months, after a series of dinners, concerts, and long conversations, the two became a couple. Teresa, profoundly lonely for several years, was not surprised when Arturo proposed. Still, she felt like a youngster again when she accepted. The couple had a traditional wedding, with an air of complete normality, and began their life together.

Arturo and Teresa's relationship was so rare that it was the subject of an article in one of Paterson's major newspapers. What the article left out, however, were a few words about the ongoing travail of others who, against their wishes, continue to live their lives alone. More often than not, these people blame themselves for not finding a partner. They torture themselves for not being interesting or attractive enough, or for not freeing themselves from their families years ago.

When they touch the center of their needs, almost all of the single men and women I have counseled want to be in love and have that love reciprocated. Unfortunately, unlike Arturo and Teresa, the older they get the less likely it is this will occur. Those who accept this can still make an effort to find the God within themselves and others, and the beauty and meaning that this search confers. Failing to do so, everything, in time, becomes essentially mundane and superfluous. In our society, as one grows older, there is a real temptation to live entirely for television, gossip, dinner, and doctors, despite the many opportunities for self-growth and service that exist.

Several years ago, when New Jersey was battered, successively, by three strong hurricanes, people whose homes were severely damaged had to be transported to shelters. The situation became desperate for homebound people and for single-parent families who depended on us to deliver food to them. Somehow our staff and volunteers were able to reach everyone in our area despite the flooding. We were also able to serve those who made it to our offices, although the food pantry was nearly bare after only four days. Volunteers, many of whom were senior citizens, restocked it completely and it continued to stay in service. There was meaning enough for all involved in this work. Those who participated, both young and old, will always be able to say that there was a storm, and that with Him, they did great things in it.

Raheed set a still-standing record for creating emergencies and disturbances at Mt. St. Joseph's Children's Center. No other youngster, among the hundreds of boys who had lived with us there, managed, in less than a month, to start so many fistfights and, on the sneak, break so many windows, sinks, and toilets with a rage and purpose indicative of untapped depths of intellect. Not yet twelve years old, Raheed was a budding social activist who attempted to organize the other children to rebel by ignoring staff's directions, refusing to attend classes, and boycotting meals with the aim of dictating future menus. Twice he climbed to the roof of the building and threatened to jump, until eventually he was helped down by firemen. He ran away from the center three times, successfully avoiding capture for at least a whole day each time. The local police found and returned him to us with increasing degrees of annoyance. They wanted to know why we didn't prevent his running.

The truth is, Mt. St. Joseph's is a home for children with emotional problems, with the emphasis on "home." It is not a correctional facility, and its staff are not guards. If children really want to run, they will ultimately find a way and time to do so. Until Raheed, this had never been much of a problem. Now he was setting an example other boys might emulate whenever something upset them. He steadfastly maintained he would keep trying until he succeeded, that soon he would leave and not be caught.

This was Raheed's best means of acting out until the day he stole a bread knife from the kitchen and announced he would kill another boy he had taken hostage, then himself. The police came and helped us disarm him. That was enough, as far as the therapists and social workers involved with Raheed were concerned. It was decided that his increasing frustration and propensity for violence would soon lead to his hurting himself or someone else. He would have to go.

What concerned us was *where* Raheed would be going. We knew he had behaved as he did because he wanted to get back home. It was his own mother, however, who had asked the state for help, because of his combative behavior, and who had agreed, with relief, to his placement with us. Our plan for Raheed was to work with him and his mother and sister to achieve exactly what he wanted: to be set free. His short stay never gave us a chance to begin rehabilitation and only confirmed his mother's feeling that he was dangerous and beyond her control. All Raheed had accomplished was to make sure his mother would not take him back. He left us and was placed in a restrictive state facility for boys demonstrably more disturbed and problematic than those we serve—a place where he was more likely to be harmed by someone bigger and tougher than he.

I was not present when he was taken by a state social worker, but I was told he was wailing, that he wanted to stay, and that he cried for his mother. The agency would make every effort that the bureaucracy would permit to relate to both mother and child, to keep telling them it was there to help at any time, no matter how long it took. Whether I am at the agency or not, should make no difference. The essence of what we do means that Raheed and his family will not be forgotten. But in that moment, I had only dark thoughts that I kept to myself. There are too many bullies out there and too many drugs. It would be all too easy for Raheed to believe he is worthless and to overreact with his hands or a weapon to prove he is not. This child needed care. Hoping and praying that he gets it are not enough. The agency had to somehow keep track of him before he is buried in the ground or buried alive in jail.

There are victims of dementia walking the streets, conversing with God, His creation, and themselves. In bad weather the police may take them to a shelter or detention center, which they leave as soon as possible. They generally reject our help, sometimes physically, sometimes just vociferously—choosing to be free of us and everyone else, to live within the mansions of their minds. We can only repeat to them where our office is and that they will be housed, fed, clothed, and protected there, should they wish. For the most part, they are able to survive on the pickings they find in refuse and the small change they receive from passersby. These people live in another place, another universe, where hunger and shelter matter less than the continuing effort to understand the visions revealed to them.

With county and state facilities either full or defunded, the profoundly mentally ill are bereft of public assistance, unless they commit a crime and are institutionalized, or deteriorate to such helplessness that the police hospitalize them against their will. Even then, they are likely to be released prematurely due to policies limiting public spending on their behalf. When this occurs they are left, once more, to survive by their own devices.

These men and women are specters in the city, appearing and disappearing almost at will, inhabiting the streets by day and retiring at dusk to those hidden enclosures of Paterson only they seem to know. What would be nightmarish for us has become tolerable for them: a barely livable, private world that few people from the outside ever enter. Our social workers persist in trying to reach them.

Some time ago, I attended what I call a "begging session." Our local legislators were considering a reduction of the state funding the agency received to prevent the eviction of marginalized people and to provide food to people in crisis. I testified, really begged, before a county board, pleading for dollars we would not be able to make up elsewhere. We would use all of the resources available to us, including the donations of our own staff, to provide food and prevent homelessness. Government's failure to support us would be disastrous. I've found that I've learned to beg quite well over the years, keeping in mind that whenever I failed, someone, somewhere in the diocese would suffer. It was a terrible but very effective incentive. A month after testifying, I learned that we had been awarded almost fifteen thousand dollars more than we had received the previous year. I was genuinely astounded. I had begged with desperate concern for those who depended on us for housing and sustenance through the coming winter. Thank God I was understood. That extra money, combined with the donations of parishioners, would make it that much easier for us to serve those who would come to us for help.

Begging has been good for me spiritually. I get too much publicity and too many accolades, too much respect from too many people that really don't know me. Begging grounds me in reality like a cancer grounds the vain and lasting pain grounds us in our finality. When I beg for funding, I ask others for their attention and consideration and, of course, expose myself to their rejection. I might very well have returned to the agency empty-handed, without the funding we needed and only the beginning of a plan to carry on.

When I first started work, I found begging very difficult. In fact, at times I could not abide it. Eventually, I was able to look forward to doing what I must. When we humble ourselves, empty ourselves on behalf of the poor, we experience some sense of our Father's love for us all. This love, felt even in its faintest intimations, is incredibly freeing. It does away with fear. Within it there is no anxiety. It makes us whole. This is a special gift to me from the people I have served, people for whom and with whom I have begged.

I made it a rule to visit the agency's adult day care programs at least twice a year. These service sites provide breakfast, lunch, and social activities as well as simple, safe, clean, pleasant environments for older people. Each time, upon my arrival, the people being served would tell me not to change their program; they liked it exactly the way it was. I would promise them that I was not a member of the Gestapo who had some secret, destructive plan in mind. At most, I would offer suggestions that they themselves could review. They swore they would hold me to my word and that the bishop would be informed should I do otherwise.

Aside from being feared as a harbinger of radical change, I generally was warmly welcomed when I visited. Those who remembered my previous visit wanted to know why it took so long for me to return. Some would inquire about my family, and almost everyone wanted to tell me about theirs. Some were silent, a few were sarcastic, while others attempted to tell me their whole life story, all the while trying to remember whether they'd done so before. These were men and women in their late sixties, seventies, eighties, and nineties. They had children in their fifties and sixties. To them, I was a youngster with a lot to learn about life and death.

A number of these people suffered from Alzheimer's disease as well as a variety of physical ailments. They played board or card games if they were able, watched television, or just talked to the staff, each other, or themselves. In a sense, they were the lucky ones who didn't comprehend their situation and, thus, were protected from the pain it entailed. They didn't care that they didn't know what day it was.

Those still mentally competent were forced to confront and deal with the disturbing circumstances of longevity. A few had outlived their spouses and their children and did not, by any means, consider that a blessing. Many lived lives consisting of trips to the bathroom, our program, the doctor, and home. They missed family and friends who had passed. Some were angry with the dead for abandoning them. Others prayed for their dead and looked forward to a joyous reunion with them. At one of my visits, a woman who was overtly disturbed asked me if I believed in the Resurrection. When I told her that I did, she started dancing and singing to the Lord, intimating that she had just converted me. What would have happened, I wonder, had I said I did not believe?

A similar incident concerned praying to Our Lady of Lourdes. A very serious woman asked me whether I knew that daily prayer to Our Lady was necessary for my personal salvation. When I said that I did not, I opened myself to a holy tirade denouncing my laziness and worldliness. Only by making immediate amends to Our Lady and promising to lead a more regimented prayer life was I able to extricate myself from her ministerial concern.

It's impossible for me not to wonder how I will react to old age, should I reach it. I already have a problem with intolerance that, if exacerbated over the years, could make me one classic, annoying, combative old geezer. Conversely, an increase in freedom from family and work responsibilities will give me more time to pray and reflect, to be less distracted. I know I'll be happy, when the end comes, to pray myself to death—if you consider our lives to be one long prayer, that's what we're all doing, silently, as best we can, in the recesses of our hearts.

Brent entered my office and announced he was probably the only homeless college student I would ever meet. He made it clear that he was not an alcoholic or drug abuser. He had never hurt anyone or been a thief. He was taking care of himself and meeting his needs except for one thing—the last two books required for the courses he was taking at Passaic County Community College. He just couldn't raise the seventy-nine dollars they cost. He showed me his college I.D. and a printout noting the books he still had to buy. If we could help him it would make all the difference. If not, he would attempt to continue borrowing the books from his fellow students. He had a strong feeling, however, that they would not tolerate this much longer.

All of this was communicated to me in a nonstop frenzy of words and gestures. Brent was so anxious and speaking so fast that I was unable to comment or ask any questions. I had to order him to stop, relax, and speak to me calmly. He never really achieved this, but he did slow down sufficiently so that we could have some kind of conversation about his problems and his plans.

Brent was twenty-two, single, and the father of no one—and he made a great deal of the latter. He was an only child who had lost contact with his natural father. After high school he worked for three years in the maintenance department of a chemical plant. Then, without notice, he was laid off. He lived on his unemployment insurance checks until they ran out. After that, he was forced to give up his apartment and move in with his mother. This arrangement lasted five months. His stepfather was an alcoholic who beat Brent's mother during his binges. Brent couldn't take it and moved into his girlfriend's apartment. His girlfriend's mother wouldn't permit this and turned him out on the street where he'd lived the past year. He soon lost his girlfriend and found he was able to get scant help from his terrified mother, who gave him twenty dollars from time to time when she thought his stepfather wouldn't notice.

In order to survive without a home, Brent constructed a very effective daily timetable, turning up at a shelter for the homeless twice a day to receive lunch, supper, and a place to sleep. He went to a church basement early each morning for breakfast and an opportunity to wash. He replenished his wardrobe from items donated to charities serving the homeless and kept his clothing in a locker provided by this church. Since beginning college, he had given up lunch, a sacrifice he was more than willing to make.

I asked Brent why he didn't secure public assistance and get a small apartment for himself. "If I take welfare I can't go to school full-time," he replied. "If I attend college full-time, my tuition is paid by the government because I'm studying a trade, computer science. I want to graduate quickly and start working. I think I'd also be lonely in an apartment. Until I get my degree, I'd rather eat and sleep with my friends in the shelters. I've never had any problems with the people there."

"Even in the winter," I asked, "when the shelters are crowded?"

"I had no trouble last winter," he said. "You just have to be polite to everyone and respect them. That's usually all it takes to get along. My only problem is that the government won't pay for my books. I can handle the rest."

Well, we had never used our emergency funds to pay for books before, and that became a problem for me. Seventy-nine dollars could purchase a lot of food for people in crisis. Brent was asking me to take a gamble on his ability to finish the two years of study required for his degree. Otherwise, this investment in his future, though small, was a loss of money that could be used to help others. I looked at the hyper young man before me and, quite frankly, felt he wouldn't make it. I doubted he could concentrate sufficiently to succeed at school. Also, his lifestyle was so fragile that it could break down at any time, making attendance at college difficult, if not impossible. His entire persona, however, was full of desire and hope. He was dead set on graduating and asked only for some minor assistance to get going. One of the recurring themes in my talks to community groups is that we must move beyond helping people get by from day to day. We must help them achieve self-sufficiency—and that's exactly what Brent was asking the agency to do. I authorized the purchase of the books he needed.

Two weeks later, Brent stopped in to show me the B+ he had received in his first mathematics exam. He said it was possible only because of the agency's help and that he would always remember how we had supported him. He was absolutely sure he would keep all the variables of his life going and graduate. He had a lock on the whole situation. Nothing was going to stop him.

Maybe that kind of conviction, I thought, will actually get him through. Stranger things have occurred in Paterson. Psalm 34:18 reads: "The Lord is near to the brokenhearted, / and saves the crushed in spirit." The Lord is also gratified, I'm sure, when a man refuses to allow his spirit to be crushed. The Lord celebrates such a man for his love of life. Brent had been struck by many sorrows. These he carefully stored away to use to create himself. I'm not sure he understands that this creation will take the whole of his life or if this matters to him at all.

She looked to be fifty or fifty-five, taking away a decade or so for the toll exacted by living homeless. Although she needed more, she accepted only five dollars and took even this as from a great distance, with the reserve and demeanor adopted by some who, in previous lives, never had to ask. She refused to tell me her name or talk about her problems or plans. She did at least have a plan, secret and sweet, because she was using the money for transportation and was determined to get started. Together, we walked two blocks to a bus stop and, when she caught her bus, she left my life.

Thirty minutes later, I was at the Chancery for a meeting of diocesan department directors. The agenda included a presentation on the fiscal woes of the diocese. I attended such meetings regularly and knew that issues that troubled me would be raised. For example, why were we repairing and restoring church buildings when there was a shortage of priests and declining church attendance? Why were we doing this when the temples of the bodies of so many people in Paterson needed immediate attention? Granted, the Chancery had more responsibilities than I did. I understood and respected this. But the five dollars given earlier that day came from money my staff donated for use in emergencies. Poor people need help, not newer, finer churches.

When I returned to the agency, it was to a planning meeting for the annual dinner, a major fund-raiser that had not been netting what it should. That year the dinner committee and I had decided to honor a popular churchman who had made some modest donations of personal time in support of our programs. For his efforts we planned to give him a plaque, a dinner, and much recognition. The idea was that his extensive contacts and acquaintances would boost attendance at the event. Now, I liked this man and appreciated what he had done, but I knew that he could readily do more. I would have to play a principle part in the award ceremony, and the sense of duplicity I felt drained me. I had done similar things in the past and was told that I'd performed well—and that's exactly what I'd done. I'd performed, acted. It was a part of my job that I thoroughly disliked.

The meeting over, I took a telephone call from the mother of a developmentally disabled man who wanted her son placed in one of our group homes. She is related to a member of the staff and uses this to ask a favor: that we place her son before others on the waiting list for admission. She is not pleased when I tell her this cannot be done. She talks about making a donation, which, I say, would be gratefully accepted but will not affect the waiting list. I do not believe I was in her prayers that night and, certainly, a check was not forthcoming. This woman had spent most of her life caring for her disabled son, as had her husband and other children. They all wanted and needed relief, and expected to get it from their church. Her disappointment was painful and justified. The obvious answer to this ongoing dilemma, of course, is to open more group homes as quickly as possible, which is what the agency was trying to do. I wished that woman could know that we would fill the city and suburbs with them if we could.

Throughout the day, I kept thinking of the woman who would accept no more than five dollars from us. Was it pride or solicitude? Was she considering the others who would come to us that day for money? Perhaps it was a mixture of both. Perhaps she had nothing in mind but getting started on her journey. In any case, she was owed thanks because others surely came.

One afternoon, an emaciated, runny-nosed, enervated woman named Cin, with a "C," you understand, came asking for money. She spun an elaborate tale of being left by her husband with four children to care for and needing cash for food and rent immediately. You could sense her disappointment when she was told we would provide her with food from our pantry, but that rental assistance was only given via a check to the landlord in question and only after written confirmation of imminent eviction. When we began talking to her about applying for public assistance as well, she was already moving toward the door. She was just about gone when we asked her to let us help her with her drug problem. We haven't seen her since.

A substantial number of the men and women in our alcohol and drug rehabilitation program, Straight and Narrow, were there only because it was an alternative to incarceration. Once in the program, they would dry out, sense their value as human beings, and graduate with jobs waiting for them. A small number, however, would return to using alcohol and drugs as soon as they could. These people beat the system by using us to stay out of jail. It was their good fortune, they believed, to have put one over on us all, right before our eyes.

It is hard to see the waste of money and resources dedicated to helping desperate people. From a Christian perspective there is, at least, the solace of knowing we have tried to do all we could for those in our charge. If at times we are played for fools, we are at least fools of Christ. This means taking addicts back into the program when they genuinely seek healing. When they really need us, they will not be attempting to avoid jail. They will have come to understand that they are attempting to avoid death.

After her short visit, I prayed Cin would come to understand the seriousness of her sickness before the inevitable occurred. I hoped she would permit herself more help than my prayers to reject the street life of an addict. I knew that should she not, should she close her arms around that life, only her sentencing or funeral awaited.

The last two weeks before Christmas were always incredibly busy at the agency. Generous parishioners throughout the diocese would donate clothing, food, and toys that would be sorted and distributed to families and individuals just as soon as they were received. The staff handled this additional work magnificently. Before their own Christmas celebrations, they would try to make sure that all who came to us for help were satisfied. It was a time of high spirits when everyone seemed especially grateful for the work we did. Then, one Christmas, just to keep our feet on the ground, Tony appeared out of the snow.

He was a thirty-year-old white man in a seriously worn jacket and dirty jeans. He was also jobless, homeless, and a victim of alcoholism. All he wanted was a place to stay for a few days and some money to buy food. The night wind and cold were the only reasons he was with us—that, and the obscure possibility of negotiating a drink. I'm not sure if he really knew exactly where he was, he just had some idea he would be helped.

Tony got agitated when we told him we could get him into Straight and Narrow. He knew all about the rehab program there and wanted nothing to do with it, even though it would provide him with food, training, and twenty-four-hour care. He started getting angry about the possibility of being really helped. What he wanted, he said, "was just a place to stay for a while and for you to keep out of the rest of my life." I told him we would honor that, but if he changed his mind and wanted treatment, to please come back. He just looked at me steadily, as if I was the biggest fool he'd ever met. For one of many possible reasons, or combinations thereof, this man thoroughly disliked me, although I had a check made out to a local hotel and personally gave it to him. Before listening to my directions to a community food program, he took the check and walked out the door without saying thank you or acknowledging any of us who had tried to help him.

Tony reminded everyone present that his world gave little cause for thanks and rejoicing. Christmas, for him, was just another time to get through. Perhaps an even more painful time than usual, what with people celebrating and exchanging greetings and gifts. He didn't have to act mannerly or like me as a person to survive, and so he didn't. It was as simple as that for him, Christmas or not.

Failure was not uncommon. We had just spent weeks getting a destitute man two jobs, clothing for work, and a small apartment for which we were prepared to pay a month's rent and security so that he could move out of the homeless shelter he lived in. He got a haircut so he would look good for his first job in over five years.

He failed to show for both jobs.

The first time, he told us there was a misunderstanding about when he was to start and the boss was unreasonable about letting him begin thereafter. We stayed with him, finding him another job. This time, without excuse, he simply didn't appear for work. We had to apologize profusely to his employer, begging for future cooperation. Semi-miraculously or very predictably, depending on one's point of view, the man reported for work at the second job three days late. He was accepted as an outright favor to us. He had temporarily canceled his plans for an apartment, deciding to remain in the shelter a while longer (a plan I strongly supported). Too many changes too fast, in a fragile and tenuous world, I thought. This man needed attention and affirmation, which meant being available to him and present for him. He was trying to create a life again, with dreams of independence, work, good food, and a pleasant place to live, all contingent upon keeping a job. He was scared about it, and I was worried and frightened for him too. Indeed, failure was not uncommon and it hurt deep, maiming hearts and personas.

A week later, one of our staff called the man's employer to see how things were going. The call was made to relieve our anxiety about his reporting to work, which he was. All of us were praying for him, although some of the staff, despite their hopes, gave odds against his succeeding. They had seen this all too many times before. Our prayers notwithstanding, they were proven correct. In less than a month, the man left the job and vanished.

A Nigerian refugee, with no small store of mental problems and no desire to address them, needed to have a heavy coat, immediately, in autumn, so great was his fear of winter in Paterson. This coat had to be a fine one, offering adequate protection in the worst weather, Arctic and beyond. His pleas were so insistent, verging on demands, that the staff conceded, understanding that this was an important issue for him, a fixation best resolved so that his other needs could be met. A good, wool Republican coat had been donated. It fit well enough to merit his approval, and he left the building wearing it.

The next day, this man returned, telling us the coat was gone. He said he had taken it off going home and thought he laid it outside the door of his apartment forgetting to bring it inside; a bounty for a visitor or fellow tenant. All he knew was that he needed another coat. We offered him one less attractive than the first, and not exactly his size, but the only one we had that was a close fit. He found the garment unacceptable, became enraged and, before departing, swore he would report us to a number of priests and civil authorities. He wanted nothing more to do with Catholic Charities, a bunch of fools and ne'er do wells.

There is some truth in what he said. There were people we could not help sufficiently despite our efforts and intentions. We could not place everyone who needed it in the decent housing they deserved. In emergencies, when our own shelters were full to capacity, we had to make referrals to public shelters. Many of the poor chose the street instead. We failed to enable people to overcome their addictions. We failed, in our counseling, to keep families together, failed the children of those families. I do not like admitting that we did not serve everyone as required, but this is so. It is a sobering, grounding truth.

If we escape desolation and depression, it is because God loves us, our failures notwithstanding. From the beginning, He knew all our weaknesses and that they are the price of our freedom; that error and frailty are part of our being, as are goodness and spirituality. My desolation subsides when I remember He cannot cease loving, but that does not mean it will never return.

Cardinal Joseph Bernardin wrote, "If the Lord experienced pain and suffering," and, I add, failure and abandonment, "can we as His disciples expect anything less?"[1] It took the Resurrection for the apostles to overcome these feelings two thousand years ago. We must trust God's love of us to overcome them today. He knows that we do not always act as we wish, and that the complexity of our personalities and the difficulties of life prevent this. I would like to retract words that I have spoken to my family and to people I have worked with. I would like to recant judgments that I had no right to make. There were times I made uneasy situations terribly worse by insisting on speaking my piece as if I had all the answers. It is part of our humanity to long to change the past and things we have done, knowing full well we cannot. It is also part of our humanity to discover we are loved just as we are, and to give of ourselves solely for the joy it brings.

Several of the staff and I attended Kevin's funeral Mass at St. John's Cathedral. He had suffered a heart attack over the weekend, alone in his apartment. Kevin was a recovering drug addict receiving treatment at the agency. He had no known family, and we had to arrange his burial in one of the plots reserved for the poor in the diocesan cemetery. His death was unexpected and, perhaps, some thought, unnecessary. The coroner remarked that if someone had been with him and the severity of the heart attack permitted, an ambulance could have been called and his life saved. This was, of course, pure conjecture. Kevin was in his early forties so some of the staff, much older than this and living alone, were given cause to consider.

Driving home from work that night, I recalled a conversation with a colleague about death. We had known each other for over eight years and had grown comfortable enough in our friendship to exchange words about our work and families. Our conversations were pleasant but never very substantive until the evening he told me he was terrified of death. His life was far from trouble free. In fact, he had endured more duress than most, but it was his life and he liked to fantasize that it would continue forever. He knew this wasn't true, both in his heart and mind, but he was so uncomfortable with death that he simply could not accept dying. People died in books and in the movies. Friends and acquaintances died. Family members died, but somehow, some way, he hoped to escape; a futile but very real desire. He acknowledged its futility. The best he could do was to sublimate the reality of death and try to appear at ease.

This man was a practicing Irish Catholic who had attended Mass since childhood. He knew the Gospels, confessed his sins, prayed to the saints, and contributed to the church. He had tried to raise his children to do the same. Yet, he could not face death.

This fear of death is genetic: an inborn, reflexive abhorrence necessary for the continuation of humanity. It is supremely natural. But what is Christianity if not a belief that wreaks havoc on the natural, a belief that teaches love and respect for the weak and directs us to sacrifice our self-interest in favor of the needs of others, a religion that teaches that the natural has been superseded by Christ, who declares the reign of death over? There is no longer anything to fear in life or death. This is the courage the early Christians lived, and the martyrs and saints thereafter. It is still the teaching that Christians are asked to live by and the reason they are called to actions that seem foolish in the eyes of the world.

I asked my colleague if he wanted to do something about the darkness that frightened him, if he would see a priest or pastoral counselor. He decided to work with a person I knew to be particularly sensitive to the issues of death and bereavement.

There is ample preparation in life for death. There are innumerable small deaths along the way. The loss of friends and family; the loss of lovers; the gradual dissipation of our abilities, mental and physical; the degradations we suffer; the realization that many of our plans are dreams that will never come to fruition; the designs we have for our children that are woven of the same fragile cloth; our periods of loneliness; the times we feel abandoned and lost in a desert of our mind's creation. These are deaths we all know. They tell us, if we are attentive, that our final death must come and that we can perdure.

I know a woman who is personally caring for her husband, the victim of a severe stroke suffered years ago. This man cannot walk without assistance, cannot cut his own food or clean himself. He speaks three words only, one of which is his wife's name. He is a big man, over six feet tall and two hundred and thirty pounds. She is perhaps five foot five and at least one hundred pounds lighter than he. Still, she has learned to maneuver her husband in and out of his wheelchair, to the shower, to bed, and to the commode. She is seventy-two years old, a year younger than her spouse, and completely able to meet his needs twenty-four hours a day. The only relief she gets from serving him is her weekly food shopping and attendance at Sunday Mass.

Over the years, I have become close to this couple. He is a good man, still eager to live despite his infirmities. His strength is grounded upon the love of his wife, a love that has grown throughout their marriage so that it now transcends her personal needs. She has died to the life she led before her husband's stroke, and has created a new life for them both, one in which love and sacrifice are indistinguishable, freely given, and gratefully accepted. Who is to say that the love they now have is not fuller than what they had before? With all defenses unnecessary, they have never known each other better and have discovered what they really require of life— each other.

This couple's greatest fear is that she will die before he does, leaving him without the care she provides. He would be taken, it is planned, to the home of one of their sons, but I doubt, in my heart, he would live long without her. I wonder how she would adjust to losing him should he die before her. Theirs is the strongest love, the most powerful bonding, I have ever witnessed, so that is difficult, almost impossible, to imagine one being without the other. Neither is afraid of death as much as they fear separation. She has told me that, against her wishes, she has begun trying to prepare for this and is asking him to begin as well, if only out of love for her. They fell in love when they were teenagers and have stayed that way as naturally as if they had been born to it. Preparing for separation is the hardest thing she has ever done; the hardest thing she has ever asked of him. She admits she is unsure he is complying; he may only be appeasing her.

Early that morning, hours before Kevin's funeral, I went outside to scan the sky for signs. I found Rigel in Orion, a cold star to my eyes, and imagined absorbing its distant heat into my bones. Without permission, the sun came, causing my star to disappear, but the reality of it persists. Like love for people who are gone.

I was involved in a love affair with a beautiful woman named Rose. Sometimes her dementia would cause her to forget me for weeks at a time, but when she remembered, she would visit my office to see how I was doing and to tell me that she loved me. She would also ask for food and for a few dollars to purchase "women's things." She was always upbeat when she saw me, trying to show she was doing well on the street.

Rose had been homeless for almost three years, following the death of her husband. She had no children or family who could help her. Twice she had been hospitalized for mental problems and twice discharged to her own care. She was on and off her medication, depending on her mood, and looked ten years older than her age of fifty-four.

Rose had strong maternal instincts, which occasionally zeroed in on me. "Why are you still single?" She would ask.

"Because I haven't found a woman I can confound and confuse into marrying me."

"These women today are crazy," she said. "I love you."

"I love you, too, Rose."

I worried about Rose's safety. My staff arranged for her to receive public assistance and once secured a room for her in a low-income housing project in Paterson. She lost the room because she refused to use it. She preferred sleeping in the downtown women's shelter or sleeping outdoors. Weather permitting, sleeping outdoors was always her preference. She liked to bed down in a small cranny of the main edifice of the diocesan cathedral. There she could be seen by only the pigeons nesting above her and by the occasional cat passing by on a nocturnal hunting foray. Rose believed that her space next to the cathedral was a holy place where God paid special attention to her prayers.

Praying, Rose will tell you, is what she does best. She prays for everyone she knows and for their families. I was a thankful beneficiary of her efforts. She prayed for me and for my father, who was wheelchair bound. Every time we met, Rose would ask if my father was walking again. When I would say no, she would assure me that she would pray even harder. I was to tell my father, for her, not to worry—he would be healed. Once Rose asked me for five dollars for something special. I gave it to her, assuming one personal need or another had arisen. Instead, she used the money to buy a small box of sweets for my father, "to lift his spirits during these difficult times." I was not to forget to tell Dad that Rose was praying for him.

When Rose was not Rose, she didn't recognize me when we saw each other on the street. In fact, she retreated from me and men in general. She would hurry away no matter how gentle my approach. When Rose was Rose, she never remembered those episodes. She just picked up the pieces of her life as if nothing at all had occurred.

I knew that something bad would eventually happen to this woman, whether she was lucid or not. She would be hurt for the price of a bottle of Thunderbird or by a drug addict who thought she was hiding more than the few dollars she actually had. She could be harmed by someone who discovered her "holy place" and wanted to use it to sleep off a drunk. She could be robbed of her few possessions, right on Main Street, in broad daylight. I would give Rose some of my business cards with my home telephone number inked in and with written instructions to call me in case of emergency. These I would strategically place in her wallet and handbag. I also asked her to put a card in one of her pockets each day. I could only hope I would be called should she be injured or hospitalized.

I never learned anything of Rose's past. She would not permit this. I was aware of her present only. There I knew a person of generosity and compassion that gave what she had to give—her prayers. Sometimes, when she would remember me, we would pray together in her holy place, "for everyone," she would say, "who has forgotten to love and for everyone whom love has forgotten." Then she would tell me, earnestly and with power, how, when, and to whom I would be married.

After years of trying to have their own child and more years of applications, interviews, hoping, praying, and waiting, an adoptive couple had finally completed the adoption process and had become parents. They came by to say it was all entirely worth it and to show us their new son. Work stopped, as it should, while we cooed at the baby who was somewhere amidst blankets and clothing; a tiny face, ten months old, alternately laughing and crying, not understanding this great attention, unsure if it was pleasing or not. He eventually tired of the faces that appeared and disappeared so quickly, and he let us know this. Time to go home, have a snack, sleep, and be loved, he said, and mother and father acquiesced. Before leaving they told me they'd sometimes thought they would never receive a child and had tried to reconcile themselves to that.

Reconcile. The word applies to everyone involved in an adoption. These new parents must be reconciled to the pain all children bring to those who love them. Will they ever regret what they have done because their son has disappointed them, and will their love overcome the mistakes he may make in their eyes?

And the child. He will have to understand the love that was surrendered by his birth parents, and grow to become loving himself. He can do this, I have seen it done, but the questions and answers about the beginning of his life will always remain. They may drive him to find his parents when he is able.

The baby's father had consented to adoption easily, without qualm. He did the right thing. At age nineteen, unemployed and looking for excitement, he was in no condition to be a parent.

It's the child's mother I worry about. She carried him, labored and birthed him. Had she wished, she could have chosen to abort. Now, she has held and fed her child, cleaned and kissed him, and let him go. It is as if he had suddenly died, but worse, because she knows he hasn't but is somewhere she can't be. She will feel pain as she watches mothers playing with their children, and in the quiet and dark when she is alone. No amount of street-talk bravado will extinguish it. There will be dreamy nights when she sees him happy and thankful for her decision, when he understands she was just too young to give him what he needed. She will have days of worry and of wishing she could change what she has done, when she wants her baby back and is angry at the father and herself and the people who adopted her child. I have great respect for her for taking this on, for having the courage not to abort. She is only a child herself, but has made a grown woman's choice.

Reconciliation. The word has a connotation that troubles me, as if meaning some settlement or agreeable adjustment between people. It should mean understanding, which is much more than that, and forgiveness, which is even more. And it can mean these things.

I know a man, adopted from an orphanage when he was three, who made up his mind when he was forty-two to find the peace he needed. When inquiries about his parents got him nowhere, he hired a private detective and turned him loose, no expense barred. He learned that his father had died but found his mother and a number of half-brothers and half-sisters and their children. He wrote them, visited them and, in effect, established a new family. He was welcomed and loved beyond expectation. He shares birthdays and holidays and vacations with them now and is always happy when he does. In no way has his love for his adoptive parents and family diminished. He is one with them and will always be, only now, he has a real past and many more relatives. Reconciliation.

Part Two

Streets and Horizons

Prostitute and junkie. The words go together naturally. Laura, the mother of an infant boy whose father is anywhere but here, readily admits these words apply to her. She told me: "I'm nowhere near the kind to raise a kid," and looked hopefully to me for a solution.

There was no room for a baby in Laura's working day of turning tricks. She had already lost clients because of the child's needs, and his demands were limiting her time to get high. Laura had neglected her child to secure the quiet she enjoyed when she was using. She wanted us to take the boy before she permanently injured or killed him. She showed no remorse or guilt at all. It was simply a matter of us relieving her of an unwanted burden so that she could continue to pursue her lifestyle of choice. She opted for adoption and told me to be sure her child was placed with a good mother.

All offers of treatment for Laura's addiction were unacceptable as far as she was concerned. She promised to look us up should she change her mind. I remember telling her that odds were she would die if she didn't do that soon. She replied, haltingly, "There's nothing wrong with dying young. There's nothing wrong with some peace." She then developed a list of things she hated with all her being. This began with men and went on to include priests, counselors, the father she never knew, the father of her child, Hispanics, black people, the government, God, and life. In the short time I knew her, she seemed constantly alert to discovering possible additions to her list.

Her baby was exceptionally beautiful and eventually was placed with a couple whose paramount wish was to have a child to care for. He may never know who his birth parents were or the circumstances of his birth. Later, these may become important issues for him. What is important now is that a life that was created by a father who vanished and a mother incapable of responsibility was entrusted to people who, in their wildest dreams, could not thank Laura and her lover more for the gift bestowed upon them.

Despite her objections, Laura is also important. God loves and cherishes her, tenderly dismissing her attempts to reject Him. She, of course, refused to believe this. There will be times when she palpably feels the loss of her son. She will ingest or inject whatever she can to avert the pain this brings. She will be affirmed in her worthlessness and will pursue annihilation with the same purposefulness with which others pursue life. If she remains adamant in refusing help, she will live the life of an isolate on the street, seeking oblivion until her wish for death is realized. When this happens, what good is there for me to know it didn't have to be?

One of the most meaningful things I have done is simply hold people who are dying of AIDS, cancer, or one of the other thousands of contingencies that take us out of life. This holding is a sign of our common humanity, a humanity that, of necessity, includes the reality of death. I've been ill and close to death myself. Perhaps those I have held sense this and take some comfort in it. At least, I know that immanent death is supremely personal and that no one can judge another's reactions to it.

I've seen critically ill people deny death with strength of purpose they never knew they had. They refuse to believe they will die, and they fight to the end for whatever additional moments of life are available. I have also seen people pass calmly, with acceptance and great equanimity. They have tolerated their tracheotomies and feeding tubes, their medications and the ministrations of doctors and nurses. All along they knew they were dying and finally they did just that.

Much has been written about near-death experiences in which people on the verge of death see a being of light and love who explains to them why they will not die. Often the reason for postponing death is the need to care for young or ill family members. Most of the people who have had this experience believe they were in the afterlife and are completely prepared to return to that experiential plane of love they briefly visited. I have little to say about this other than it certainly would be wonderful, if true.

No one can say exactly what happens after death, but Christians can say that whatever it is, it is love upon love. Our faith is centered upon the fact that our Father always cares for us. This is why, when ministering to the dying, we can address the fear and guilt they may understandably feel. One man, dying of cancer, was sure beyond doubt he was going to hell because his gambling and alcoholism left him nothing to leave his wife and child. I assured him we would care for his family. Over and over again, we discussed the parable of the prodigal son until he realized God had already forgiven him before he had even thought to ask. Over and over again, we discussed the immeasurable love God has for each of us, sinners that we are. He hugged me a few days before his death and said there was nothing to fear. By hugging him back, as hard as I could, I was saying the same thing.

It is early 1998—two years until the end of the millennium, but certain celebratory activities had already begun. This particular morning, a tall, gaunt prophet with too serious a face stopped me on the street and gave me a flyer meant to prepare me for the ominous event. I read that, when the great day comes, the Son of Man will appear on the clouds of heaven with power and glory. He will dispatch His angels who will assemble the saved. There will be wailing and grinding of teeth as the wheat is separated from the chaff. I am advised that now is the time to repent—or risk being caught unaware at the time of judgment, which will be precisely on the midnight second of December 31, 1999.

I am no longer able to summon enough irrational, interior fear to be impressed by such certainty. If someone doesn't start a nuclear war before then, the moment will come and pass like the others preceding it, except that the media will make something of it for a while. Then they will move on, focusing their attention on the next interesting crime or scandal. What will the tall prophet say when the magic time comes and passes? Perhaps he will preach that we have been spared by God until the year three thousand. I had a feeling that part of him was dying for us all to expire, that he couldn't wait to see what would happen to the chaff.

Two local, more immediate events occurred that were, for me, of greater import than any portents of universal calamity. One day, the mail brought a letter from a woman who had received rental assistance from us two months earlier. Since then, she had found a job as a typist and was earning enough money to get by. Her employer had offered her training in computer literacy, which she would begin soon. She wrote that the money we gave her had made all the difference. It kept her out of a homeless shelter and let her find work without the disruption that eviction would have caused. Folded in the letter were three ten-dollar bills for the poor.

My next surprise was delivered by a well-dressed young man on his lunch break. His father had recently died, and his father's wheelchair, which was in mint condition, was of no use to anyone he knew. He gave it to me with the understanding that I'd make sure it went to someone who really needed it. While thanking him, I told him that this was an easy requirement to meet. I already had someone in mind; an elderly woman who was living with an antiquated chair and who would be delighted by that one. It had been a problem we were just about to address, and then it was solved.

I am nourished by all this generosity. It helps ground me in the gospel to know the poor are still remembered and that there is a living body of Christians who take their religion and responsibilities seriously. When the Church first started, those who became Christians gave all they had to the new movement. They lived in community, each sharing their belongings with the others, each being cared for as needed (see Acts 4:32–35). The giving I saw that day was a continuation of the spirit of those times. It wasn't as organized a charitable effort as in Acts, but it was as purposeful and personal. Some of us are still trying, after two thousand years, to live as Christians. In the midst of our trying, it is not possible to worry about millenniums. It is enough to offer what we can, one day at a time.

On one of those bitter cold March mornings that no one abides, a well-built black man in his thirties was in the agency waiting room. He had come in late and was way down the interview list, but patiently waited his turn. When that occurred, he told the caseworker assigned to him a short, hard story about his life and his simple, single need. His name was Thomas.

He was an unemployed teamster presently living on the street. He ate and slept in homeless shelters when necessary, preferring to be outdoors whenever possible. He had lost his wife, child, and job to a cocaine addiction he swore he'd rehabbed from two years earlier. All he wanted of us was forty dollars to buy a new pair of sneakers that were on sale downtown. With these he could at least look for work. The sneakers he was wearing were totally destroyed. In truth, they looked more like sandals than shoes.

The agency seldom gave people money to buy new clothing, so this purchase of sneakers required approval. When his caseworker, Vilma, asked me to see Thomas's shoes, I balked at first. It was a busy morning and I didn't want to look at sneakers. I would take her word for it and authorize the payment. "But just come for a second," she said. I did, and made sure Thomas got the money quickly. He was so grateful he gave Vilma a huge hug and thanked me profusely, swearing that as soon as he could he would repay us so that other people could be helped.

I have to admit, I put no credence in the man's promise, figuring the odds of repayment being about a thousand to one. A lot of people promise to do this when they receive help from us. Very few actually come through. It means nothing really. Imagine living day to day without a job and home, or with a low-income job and a paper-thin budget. It's easy to forget promising to part with extra money the rare times you have it. I felt more than paid back by the thanks this man expressed from his heart and by the hug he had given. That hug meant we are all in this together and that sometimes things can turn out right despite the strange and terrible circumstances of our lives.

Thomas came back to show us his new sneakers and to discuss the plans he could now pursue. He said he felt terrific. When we asked if we could help him in any other way, he said no, he could handle himself on the street. We never heard from him again.

The sounds of five boisterous, combative children, each struggling to posit their existence in the universe, are what first drew my attention to Alma. She and her angels descended on the agency like paratroopers and let everyone know they'd landed. She told us she was twenty-nine, Puerto Rican and, but for the children, essentially alone in the U.S. Two of her children, her firstborn sons, were developmentally disabled. During their entire lifetimes they had received no rehabilitative services. Alma was panicking because her common-law husband, Marco, who for years had been drinking, drugging, and womanizing like a crazed vaquero, had left her with no means of support. Even though he had abandoned her, she remained terrified of his temper and possible drunk or drugged return. She showed me a three-inch scar on her left hand where he cut her during their last disagreement. It was deep and would be life long. He had been gone for four months, and she'd learned to do without his charming personality.

Later that afternoon, one of our staff examined Alma's apartment and returned appalled. It consisted of two rooms and a bathroom. There was peeling paint and rat feces wherever you looked. Alma was paying four hundred and ten dollars a month to shelter herself, her children, and two or three families of rats. She had used up her small savings and would soon be evicted and referred to a public shelter. In this instance, our worker thought the shelter would be a step up.

Because Marco had left no clue to his whereabouts, the issue of his contributing to child support was moot. The severe disabilities of two of the children, however, meant that Alma could receive a considerable monthly stipend over and above the welfare assistance available to her as an unemployed mother. This was enough for her to find a decent apartment and still have adequate funds for food and clothing. Within a month, she had a four-room apartment she could afford. We helped her with furniture and appliances. We enrolled her disabled children in our own special needs program, and made sure the other children were properly registered in school.

We also secured a court order of protection barring Marco from bothering her in the future.

For a while Alma worried about a surprise appearance by Marco. One thing she knew for sure was that he would not surprise her with support for his children or attempt to attend to their emotional needs. For decades, a salient point made by sociologists studying urban problems is that too many men simply refuse responsibility for their families. The attention of mothers, aunts, uncles, and grandparents is more often than not insufficient to make up for the absence of a child's father. This absence is as great a plague in our communities today as the addictions and crimes that receive so much publicity. An unacceptable number of fathers have somehow come to believe that they can turn their backs on their children, that it is permissible to start a family and then move on when things get uncomfortable.

I have a fantasy that these fathers in absentia are gathered up and sent, one by one, to a place resembling the Alaskan high arctic. There, without any companionship, under psychically and physically painful circumstances, they are forced to discern ways to survive without guidance and support. They have to sleep in the snow until they find shelter or learn to make it. They starve until they grasp, all by themselves, the ways to fish and hunt. They remain naked until they understand the use of skins for clothing. From time to time, they meet bigger, stronger men who take away what little they have. By suffering so, they will understand the pain of the mothers and the children they deserted.

I once received a very different Christmas gift. It was a bookmark with the following words inscribed on it: "We cannot know what God knows, but we can know what He's forgotten." With this gift came an anonymous note that said: "Merry Christmas, from one sinner to another." You don't get many gifts like that.

I showed the bookmark to members of my family, to friends, and to colleagues at work to see their response. Some people who were tired of their problems and angry about them, said, "Sure, I know what He's forgotten. He's forgotten us." Most people understood the words to mean that God had forgotten their sins. They said they hoped it was true, but doubted it was.

When I was visiting my father in the hospital after his stroke, I became friendly with the man in the bed next to his. My father had lost the ability to speak and slept most of the time, so it was only natural and polite to talk to this man, Robert, during visits. He was recovering from a severe heart attack and knew that his lifestyle would have to change radically to avoid another episode. He also knew that another heart attack could well be fatal. This didn't seem to bother him much at all. One day, when I commented on his composure, he told me why.

Robert had been in the D-Day landing during World War II. He was an infantry sergeant with responsibility for a squad of nine men. Immediately after landing on Omaha Beach, his platoon was pinned down by artillery and mortar fire. The barrage was so thick it was absolutely impossible for them to move. Robert said it was the most incredible, memorable experience of his life. He had his whole face, eyes closed, pushed into the loose rock he was laying on, as he waited to be destroyed. He didn't cry out. He wasn't angry. He didn't pray. He just waited. When the barrage slackened, he rose and ran for cover up the beach. When he finally regrouped his squad, there were only two men left.

"Do you understand now why I'm not afraid to be here?" he asked.

"God bless you for going through all that," I said.

"That's another thing," he said. "I'm sure God blessed all of us that day—the men who made it and the men who didn't. That might sound strange, but that's what I think happened." When I showed him the bookmark at a later visit, he said, "Yes, that's what I mean. All our sins were forgotten and all of us were somehow blessed. It took the war to make me see how big God really is."

I showed the bookmark to a young man with AIDS who attended one of the agency's HIV programs. "Yes," he said, "I completely agree with this. We discuss forgiveness all the time in the program. This is about God loving us so much He has forgotten our sins or trespasses or whatever you want to call them. It's true, thank God." This was said with genuine conviction.

During my life, I've done my share of sinning. Knowing this, and admitting it, is the reason why the parable of the prodigal son speaks so meaningfully to me. I know many people with AIDS who use this parable to get them through the hard days of their lives. Several of the men and women who are being treated for alcohol and drug addiction also use it at difficult times. Many of them plan to use the parable to help them through their deaths. In essence, they are saying, we know what God has forgotten and can start forgetting it ourselves.

Paulette was one of the most beautiful women I have ever met—jet-black hair, perfect features, striking gray eyes, and a gorgeous physique. She was in her late thirties, a college graduate with a degree in political science, happily married to a successful contractor. She had two healthy sons and all the money she needed. She professed she enjoyed her life as a mother and housewife and did not want a career. She was active in her community and parish, serving on voluntary committees, singing in the church choir, and helping with parish fund-raising. Many envied the pleasant life she seemed to lead.

Her life might have been pleasant, except that for three or four days each month, Paulette would suffer a powerful depression. She did her best to hide what she was feeling but eventually, during her "bad times," she withdrew so deeply into herself that her husband had to act. He sought the advice of his pastor, Monsignor Royce, who referred Paulette to Catholic Charities. After seeing one of our social workers and a physician who specializes in depressive disorders, Paulette was prescribed medication that not only made her feel normal, but well. She was amazed that medication could help her so quickly. One day, when speaking to me about her recovery, she said, "I know I've been saved for my family." When I tried to discuss the value of her saving herself for herself, she demurred. It was about a month later that she asked if she could talk to me.

Paulette began by describing her bouts of depression, which had begun in her mid-twenties. She said experiencing them was like "being at sea." "There is an infinitely distant horizon around you, completely empty," she said. "In this place there are no markers, there is no meaning or purpose. There is no reason to care for anyone or worry about anything. Nothing matters. Absolutely nothing matters, especially your own efforts. The efforts and concerns of others are also ludicrous. Your family is baggage that is dragging you to the grave with their ceaseless, meaningless demands. And what of God, the God that so much is spoken of and written about? That's the question. There is no manifestation of God that you can see. No word of God to hear. There is only the story of God, developed over the ages to mollify our fears. God is absent. If He exists, this absence toward those who pray to Him is criminal. Who wants to know such a God?"

"Sooner or later," Paulette said, "come the inevitable thoughts of suicide. These are not frightening. On the contrary, they are beautiful, consoling thoughts. They hold, after all, the certitude of a surcease of pain. As the disease progressed, it became easier and easier to accept suicide as the best answer to my problems. I really wanted out of life. My only thought was to stop the dull, merciless pain of living that now was always with me. I started to buy all of the barbiturates I could. When I had more than two hundred, I was going to do it. That amount of drugs would certainly kill me. What stopped me were the boys. I just couldn't leave them without a mother, bad a one as I might be. I agonized over it for weeks. Finally, I promised myself I would end my life just as soon as I thought the boys were able to care for themselves. Then, Monsignor Royce sent me to Charities for help and, with the medication prescribed for me, I'm incredibly better. It was foolish of me to wait so long to seek help, but I was embarrassed about having mental problems. I came to see you to say thank you for everything Charities has done for me. I feel I've been saved from murdering myself and from hurting my family. I've been given a second chance to be the wife and mother I know I really am."

Four years later, Monsignor Royce told me that Paulette had committed suicide. She died of carbon monoxide poisoning in her spotlessly clean car in her orderly garage, a few months after her youngest son had turned eighteen.

Paulette had assiduously attended her therapy sessions and was purportedly taking her medication. Obviously, her second chance was insufficient and, despite the help she received, she remained vulnerable to a final, devastating depression. Lost and alone on her meaningless sea, she followed the compulsion to bring her life to an end. She left a note to her husband begging his forgiveness and asking him to tell the boys about the pain that consumed her. She said in the note: "I need the great peace of death. If there is a God, He will understand this and forgive."

I do believe God will forgive Paulette and embrace her in His love. The forgiveness of her family, however, will not come so easily. She has irrevocably changed their lives, abandoning them to their own devices, without the love and warmth they looked to her to provide. They will recall her on family occasions and during personal moments of solitude and recollection. During those times, her need for the great peace of death will be reflected upon in anger, sorrow, and resignation. I've learned that her grandchildren to come will be told she was stricken with cancer and that she lived and died a saint.

Most people underestimate the role chance plays in their lives. An infinitesimal genetic change means you are crippled, deaf, or blind while your brothers and sisters are not. You leave work one minute earlier or later, and you avoid an automobile accident that could have taken away your legs. You guess correctly on two exam questions, and you enter law school instead of working in the family business. You arrive just in time to buy the only bad dose of smack from your dealer, and you're dead. The earth circles the sun closer or farther than it actually does, and life cannot develop on the planet.

A number of people, deep in their hearts, wish we had never appeared on the planet anyway. All we have inherited, they say, is suffering and pain—and the legacy we leave our children is the same. The best we can do is accept the universe that has been forced upon us as reasonably as we can and try to remain detached, amused, or distracted.

The pain these people so acutely feel is everyone's at one time or another. It is part of our humanity to doubt God's providence and question the efficacy of creating a universe at risk. It is not a sin or something to be embarrassed about. In fact, I think God would be disappointed in us were we to do otherwise. Perhaps it is how we live and love, despite it all, that endears us so to Him.

During the summer, I become one of the many people who visit supermarkets on the weekend, not so much to shop as to enjoy the air-conditioning. One Saturday afternoon, I passed my cart by an elderly woman who was in deep conversation with a young man, perhaps in his middle twenties. The slowness of his responses to the shopping directions she gave him evinced some sort of mental disability. He was concentrating hard and giving her his complete attention. I thought for sure he was the woman's son or relative, but I was wrong. When I asked her how things were going, she said, "Fine, just like every time we do this." She told me she and the young man lived in the same apartment building and had become friends. She shopped with him every Saturday to make sure he had food for the week. He chose what he wanted with her looking on, paid for it with her watching, and carried both his and her food home. They had shopped together for years and were very happy with the arrangement. She said it didn't bother her if it took two or three hours to shop this way. He lived alone and if she didn't help him, who would? A very simple story about truly great love.

Christianity is essentially a religion of opportunity—of opportunities to "be there" for each other. The love that is created when people care for others is what God grasps and holds in the essence of His being. God will preserve this and sustain it after the sun expands and swallows the earth, and after the energy of the last star has burned so that there is total night. Our Father, Who guarantees this, is darkness and light and more.

One morning, a young couple, confused and disoriented, wandered tentatively into the office. They were from Las Vegas and, while visiting friends in New York, their purse and wallet had been lifted in Grand Central Station. Gwen was four months pregnant and consistently supportive of her husband's decisions, regardless, it seemed, of their practicality. Alan was extremely protective of her, but out of his league in dealing with the situation they were in. He decided they should hitchhike back to Nevada, begging food along the way. Paterson was as far as they got. Gwen had no family she could count on. Alan had a mother in Las Vegas who would let the couple live with her but, being on welfare, hadn't the resources to pay for their return.

These poor people had no idea where they were. A ride dropped them off on Route 80, and they were in Paterson, a place they had never heard of. They hadn't a clue how to hitchhike from New Jersey back to Nevada. They were hungry and thirsty, and feared they were harming the child they were expecting. They were both unemployed and had no credit cards or bank accounts. They had undertaken their trip, via one-way bus tickets, as a short hiatus from the poverty they expected to endure for some time to come. The friends they visited had many children but little cash and were unable to part with what extra money they could raise. The couple's inability to secure any kind of assistance was maddening, considering the precautions they had taken. They had made sure, all through their six-day visit, that they kept enough cash to purchase return tickets. Gwen never put her purse down and Alan kept his wallet in his back pants pocket—but it made no difference. Gwen was ripped off with such astounding finesse that, for some seconds, she simply couldn't react. When she did, the thief had speed and moves enough to disappear despite her shouts. Later, when Alan reached for his wallet, he found an empty pocket. It was a perfectly executed double play performed by people whose lives depend on doing it right. New York, New York, a wonderful town, where the rubes are discovered and shook down.

The couple also wasn't exactly sure who we were. They were walking the streets looking for directions and shelter, when they saw the word "Catholic" on the sign in front of the building. Being at least nominally Catholic, they entered, hoping some priest would be able to rescue them.

When I met them, I could see they were disappointed about something. It was later they told me it was because I wasn't ordained. Nevertheless, they described their situation as best they could, adding that although they didn't attend Mass, they prayed regularly, not only for themselves but also for the general well-being of us all.

The agency was able to provide Alan and Gwen with bus fare back to Las Vegas, and with money for food during the three-day trip. They interpreted all of this as miraculous, saying it was certainly the Lord's will that they found us in this strange and obscure place. After expressing their thanks, they were back on their way to the desert.

The genuine naiveté of these two children of God was beautiful but dangerous. They were easy prey in a city like New York. The whole concept of vacationing in New York while on welfare is questionable, not to mention their plan to hitch rides all the way home. Conversely, the intensity of their love for each other was quietly evident in all they said and did. It was what kept them sane in this world—and would not readily be surrendered. In five months' time they would have to begin integrating the birth of new life into their relationship, sculpting it, molding it into the best fit possible for themselves and their child. After being together for four years and dreaming of starting a family, they felt they were ready. What they needed was a job for Alan. Perhaps I should have hired him to represent the agency at public funding meetings where insanity rules and the freest of free spirits seem to win the day. I've seen people get funding at these meetings for projects they knew nothing about that were located in places they'd never been. Given his vast experience with disorientation, Alan could certainly do no worse.

Arlene, age seventeen, tired mother of an infant boy, came to us with a major but not uncommon problem. It is winter and she has spent all her welfare money on food and clothing. She is two months behind in her rent and has been threatened with eviction. She has no family to turn to for help; they are on welfare themselves. The child's father disappeared immediately after holding and kissing his progeny. She is petrified, angry at all men, and reaching out for any way to avoid having to live in a shelter. She talks about killing herself and her baby. She presents me with her eviction notice as if it were a papal decree.

Arlene's rent is $310 per month, and I begin thinking about which social worker we have who can quickly find shelter for her or help us raise the money for her back rent. That would be Joan Tyler. I asked Joan to start working with our staff attorney to see what could be done.

What could be done, it turned out, was substantial. Joan visited the apartment and found water running down a wall in the kitchen, a water-soaked carpet in the living room caused by the problem in the kitchen, and peeling paint in all three rooms of the apartment. Photos were taken of the peeling paint, the carpet, and the wall.

At the eviction proceeding, these photos as well as Joan's and Arlene's personal testimonies, were presented. The judge ruled that no rent need be paid the landlord until such time as the apartment was made habitable. The back rent was paid to the court to be held in escrow until then. The agency contributed $400 to the cause and two other local agencies gave $120 each. The eviction, at least, had been forestalled, but we could not commit to paying Arlene's rent indefinitely.

What we could do was give her and the baby all the food they needed and provide some donated clothing. Joan found that Arlene could receive an additional $108 per month from welfare, which was hers just for the asking. Arlene simply never knew about this entitlement. Joan and Arlene developed a budget based on her increased welfare payments and our helping her with food. If honored, this budget would permit Arlene to meet her rent and utility payments and have some money for other living expenses. She would not have a telephone.

Six days after the court ruling, Arlene's apartment was declared habitable. The landlord's workmen had actually done a good job. Arlene could not believe what had happened and how quickly it had occurred. It blew me away—a teenager with a tiny child, no family to help her, living one day at a time, so thankful for anything positive that happened in her life. She herself an adolescent who was no longer allowed to act like one. She was learning to be a woman and a mother.

Arlene had reached out to men for safety and security with disastrous results. She had sought government assistance that proved inadequate. She had looked to her family and was rejected. After all that, she was not about to let go of anyone who had helped her. We all knew she was going to hold on tight to us and that we would have to make time to accommodate her needs. That proved to be time well spent. Arlene decided to go back to high school and get her diploma. We were able to care for her child at one of our infant day care centers while she did this. She graduated two years after we first met. At age nineteen, we hired her as a childcare worker at one of our downtown day care centers, allowing her to get off welfare and move into a nicer apartment in a better part of Paterson. Our decision to employ her was one of the best we've made. She has been admirably conscientious and treats the children in her care as if they were her own. She plans to attend William Paterson College when her baby is older.

When I was a child, I often slept at my grandmother's apartment in the Bronx because my parents worked late establishing their business. I loved staying at Grandma's because she out-and-out spoiled me, and because I could spend time with my uncle, John, who lived with her. Uncle John was a New York City Correction's Officer and a combat veteran of World War II. He always told great stories about his prison work and even better ones about his experiences in the war. He had two Purple Hearts from the fighting in France and patiently, over and over again, showed me the scars where a bullet, and then shrapnel, had entered his leg and been removed. He kept his army uniform, with staff sergeant's stripes and campaign medals, in his dresser, along with a German Lueger and a Nazi officer's sword he had brought home as trophies. He was a hero of giant proportion to me, not only because of his medals and stories, but also because of what I saw and heard happening to him many times at night.

My grandmother, in whose room I slept, was quite on in years and, once out for the night, heard nothing. But not I. I listened to my uncle moaning, then speaking in anxious phrases, cursing Germans and other people, directing fire, giving orders to men, sometimes wailing and crying. I would sneak out of bed and peek in on him. He would be moving all over the bed, covered with sweat, living out his dreams. Today we call my uncle John's nightmares *post-traumatic stress disorder*, a term unknown to us then. He just said he had "the nerves," and accepted them as another wound of war. He never sought treatment of any kind and, as far as I know, suffered this way until his death.

Seeing my uncle live through the torture of so many nights gave me some preparation others didn't have when, much later, veterans of Vietnam described their pain. Like John, they had killed men and had seen their comrades killed. They had seen men's hands and feet, arms and legs, blown away. Some were paraplegics themselves. They had witnessed civilians—women, children, innocent men, and elders—maimed and killed. At times, they had lived, hour by hour, with their lives hanging by a thread, their only desire being to get home as soon as possible, alive and whole. There was a difference, however, in their stories and my uncle's—burdens they carry that my uncle, for all he went through, was spared.

Vietnam was the first war in the experience of twentieth-century Americans in which our side was not clearly, beyond question, the "good guys." Whether he merited it or not, Ho Chi Minh never attained the villainous status so evidently attributed to Hitler, Mussolini, and Hirohito. As the years went by and our casualties mounted to no effect, it became ever more difficult to justify our involvement. Reports of atrocities committed by the South Vietnamese Army and our own troops made the situation worse. There were significant protests against the war from the late sixties on and, at its end, there was, and still is, a sense of shame about what happened. This shame determined the attitude of many of us toward the men who fought the war. There are some who would like to forget them and the scars they bear, focusing instead on the victors of Grenada and the Gulf War. They prefer to pretend that Vietnam didn't occur and that its veterans don't exist. The men who fought there are not respected like my uncle was. They have been relegated to the status of phantoms.

To become ghosts before their time is not what these men imagined would happen. They were almost all draftees, very young, and admittedly afraid. They prosecuted war the way they thought they were supposed to, or were forced to. They served their country and its prevalent national policy—and were then asked to quietly disappear because that policy was found bankrupt. They continue to receive money from the government in lieu of lost limbs and damaged psyches, but balk at paying the price many would exact for this largesse: that they conveniently vanish.

The men I have talked with all suffer serious physical or mental wounds from the war. Some of them are without hope of being in love, of having children, or ever working meaningfully again. They ask, sarcastically and dreadfully, how it is they are so lucky as to have no luck at all? Most are in support groups; many have tried or are in psychotherapy. They have been prescribed Mellaril, Lonopin, Tegretol, Depakote, Prozac, and more—drugs that make time bearable for a while but are not cures. The nightmares still find ways to come, and the sense of being betrayed by their leaders and countrymen remains.

I opposed the Vietnam War, participating in marches and demonstrations against it nearly the whole time it was waged. I remember having less than warm feelings for the men who were sent there. I was still young enough to believe that they all should have refused to go. Some growing on my part was necessary for me to see it was not that simple. It is long past time when these soldiers should be welcomed as survivors of a horror that those of us who escaped can only imagine. Before our generation passes, we should let them know that we appreciate what they were made to sacrifice. *Appreciate* is a word they often use in our conversations, as well as the word *respect*. They can't grow new limbs and they tire of doctors and medications, but they never tire of respect and appreciation honestly offered, or of any sign that means they haven't been forgotten.

Veterans' reactions to their experiences in Vietnam are as diverse and personal as one would expect. For some, the value of life was cheapened while others came to see all life as precious.

Salvatore and I were friends from high school who shared, besides other interests common to boys in their teens, a love of fishing. We went blue fishing in party boats on Long Island Sound before he was drafted and served a tour of duty in Vietnam in 1969. When he returned we did some celebrating, paying our respects to old, friendly bars we knew in Manhattan. He talked about his part in the war and the trouble he was having adjusting to being home. He heard voices at night and had visions of incidents he wanted to put behind him.

Eventually our conversation turned to fishing and the way we both got started. Like most men, we shared a similar history about catching fish. As youngsters we brought home absolutely everything we caught to show our parents and friends, to prove our manhood, our worthiness, who knows? When we grew older we learned to keep only the fish we would eat, and to release the rest. This is the stage I'm still in. Since the war, Sal said he couldn't bring himself to hook a fish in the mouth and kill it. He didn't see the sport in it anymore. Instead, he liked to go to a pond near his home and throw bread to the carp and sunfish there, watching them rise and take the food he gave. He said it was very relaxing, good for the soul, and he invited me to go along. I did and found he was right. I still went fishing though and, to his credit, Sal did not permit this to interfere with our friendship.

In the late 70s, Sal got married and moved to Ohio. We gradually lost touch with each other as so easily happens. He did write me once, however, saying he had found another pond as peaceful as the last.

A stunning dream: I was in a forest so blue and green that the fairest lands I've ever seen paled in comparison. I was walking, with others, on a pilgrimage to see the Lord. We were tremendously excited about finally being with Him. Some of us wondered if we had died. No one really knew.

We came to a clearing and began to prepare a feast. Everyone in the party was ravenously hungry. He appeared before the first taste of lamb was taken, the wounds in His hands and feet visible, but healed. At His signal we partook of the lamb with a sense of joy and celebration. He said, "Eat, for with each morsel, a million can be fed and a million more again. The time of hunger has ended."

This dream was clearly a carryover from work, an obvious wish-fulfillment fantasy. But it impressed me and before leaving for the office that morning, I jotted it down in a notebook.

That day, I chaired yet another director's meeting at which the need for more staff and more funding was expressed; I participated in a state review of our programs for senior citizens, which would determine whether our request for expansion of these programs would be honored; I returned a telephone call from Washington, D.C., headquarters of the Campaign for Human Development, regarding the viability of a proposal submitted to them by one of our local organizations; and I met with a pastor who wanted to lease property to us to ameliorate his parish debt. While I kept busy, the agency staff was responding to people whose faces are different but whose needs seem the same, day after day:

A sixty-nine-year-old gentleman's apartment has burned. The fire has taken all his possessions. Can we help relocate him and supply him with food and clothing? Of course.

A twenty-six-year-old woman has fled her abusive husband. Can we find shelter for her and her two children and help her apply for public assistance? No problem.

A twenty-year-old prostitute wants to kick drugs and start a new life. Can we find shelter and a drug rehabilitation program for her? Absolutely.

A seventy-year-old woman's husband has died. She has no idea how to live without him. Is there anyone she can talk to? Certainly.

Two very young, intoxicated men are demanding money for food. They are told to come back when they're sober and we'll talk about their real needs. We will not waste money prolonging their binges.

    During the day, over forty people came requesting food or emergency rental assistance to prevent evictions. Most of them were senior citizens or women with children. Somehow, we were able to help them.

    That evening, I gave a talk to a parish group interested in the work of the agency. When I finished, I made the customary request for donations of food and money. They promised to give both, God bless them.

    That night, before rest, I thought of all those we had served that day in Paterson alone. *My God, how much more pain must occur? How much more suffering must be endured? How can we, in this nation, stand before You unashamed by our behavior to our brothers and sisters, young and old, who ask only for that which we say, in our own manifestos, they are entitled to: food, clothing, shelter, and respect? These they should have without resorting to Catholic Charities.*

    That night, before sleep, I asked the Lord to help me remember that I'm no better a person than any of those who need our help. I asked for the poverty of spirit and patience our work requires. I confess, I also fantasized about returning to the beauty and peace of that forest and feast I had dreamt of. In my moments of utmost sanity, I want to attend that feast forever.

When John Stile walked into the agency's waiting room and was interviewed by Jorge Caldera, one of our staff, we had no idea his story would be featured in the diocesan newspaper. What we knew for certain was that he was sixty-seven years old, had been homeless for over two years, and was desperately seeking help. He stated, honestly and repeatedly, that he could not go on this way.

John was an exceptionally articulate man and was able to describe his problems clearly and in detail. He had worked as a technical writer under contract to IBM and several other firms. Because he worked under contract, he did not access the pension programs of the corporations that paid him. When his services were no longer needed and he couldn't find another job, he became dependent on the slim income he received from Social Security and his VA Disability Pension. Eventually his home was foreclosed and sold for nonpayment of taxes. He had depleted his savings to pay his utility and food bills. Incredibly, after years of labor, he was homeless.

John took residence in the Alexander Hamilton Hotel in Paterson, which charges $130 per week for a single room. This sum was too great for him to meet on a regular basis. During the times when his Social Security and veteran's money ran out, he sought refuge in the various emergency shelters operating in the city. These provided him a place to sleep at night, but required him to leave early each morning. John was then on the street, waiting for his checks to arrive again so that he could rent a room for a while at the hotel. Some two years of this, for a man of his age, had taken a tremendous toll, evident in the lines on his face and the slow, careful way he walked. He had been approached by crack dealers, drug addicts looking for money, pimps, prostitutes, and the emotionally and mentally disturbed. Nothing in his education or background had prepared him for these encounters. Somehow he had survived, albeit making some serious mistakes along the way.

One salient error was stating that he "felt like killing" the judge who made the foreclosure decision on his home. This resulted in his serving eight months in jail for making a death threat to a member of the judiciary and his being put on three years probation. Eight months in jail for, at that time, a sixty-five-year-old man, had seemed impossibly long.

His next mistake was a brief encounter with crack cocaine. Some street friends turned him on for free, and he sensed he'd become addicted almost immediately. He went to an outpatient rehab program at a VA hospital until he felt normal again.

Free from his legal and cocaine problems, John's remaining worry was the continuing, periodic homelessness caused by the paucity of his income. That's when he came to the agency and began working with Jorge Caldera. John told Jorge that for over two years he had attempted to secure an apartment in one of the buildings operated by the Paterson Housing Authority. This was a dream he believed was dead. He had made applications and pleas to the Disabled American Veterans, the Veterans Administration, the Paterson City Council, the Mayor's Office, his congressman and assorted other officials. He had gotten absolutely nowhere with these efforts. Jorge made one telephone call to a contact he has at the Housing Authority—and a studio apartment at one of the Authority's senior citizen complexes was made available. Jorge said about his contact, "He has a good heart," refusing to take any credit for his own networking ability, developed over nineteen years of working cooperatively with people and agencies in Paterson.

Jorge was in his early sixties and had just about seen it all. Yet, instead of growing distant or becoming irascible, as some social workers do, he remained remarkably patient and gentle with his clients. He had never experienced burnout as far as I knew. He worked with the persistence and energy of those who believe helping others is what Christianity is about. With genuine humility he never sought recognition for what he did. Once, I asked him to receive the agency's Caritas Award, which he certainly deserved. The vehemence with which he turned me down ensured I would never ask again. Still, I wanted him to receive some recognition for all he'd done, and I had an idea that might be acceptable to him.

One morning, after John had settled in his new home, I asked him and Jorge if they would consent to be interviewed by the diocesan newspaper. I explained they would be doing the agency a great favor by helping us reach people who are not aware of our work. John had no problem with this and Jorge, after balking a bit, agreed to participate for the good of the agency.

Two days later, a reporter and photographer from *The Beacon* came to cover the story, which, subsequently, three weeks later, appeared on page one. The headline, much to Jorge's chagrin, read "Miracle Worker—Catholic Charities Aide Knows How To Cut Through Red Tape."

All of us who worked with Jorge, and had seen him help people like John over the years, knew he was able to make "miracles" happen on a regular basis. What the newspaper didn't know was that most of the staff did something miraculous just about every day. They may not have the contacts Jorge does, but they have his dedication and sense of mission.

Why were John's requests for help from governmental entities fruitless? I believe it is because many of the social workers he met there assist people only because they are paid to. They have stopped caring about people in their hearts. After an eight-hour day, too many of them go home and entirely forget about their work, regardless of whether a bit of extra effort, after working hours, would have made a real difference to someone. Some of them don't like their jobs, which makes it even harder for them to be helpful. Too many people working in government offices become so inured to pleas for assistance that they no longer see clients as people. They regard them as "units" that must be categorized according to officially defined standards. These standards determine who receives help and who doesn't and how much assistance will be given to those who qualify. If you fail to qualify, good-bye.

People working in the offices of elected officials apply a different criterion. They want to know if a person they help is going to vote, and they are well aware that homeless or helpless people don't. Generally, the best a nonvoter can expect is a referral to someone or someplace else.

The reason Catholic Charities receives the support and applause it does is because people like Jorge Caldera make the needs of others their paramount concern and keep working until these needs are met. This means that long hours, with no overtime pay, are accepted as routine. Overtime is recompensed by change for the better, one person at a time. Government workers find this threatening and revolutionary, and they are right to do so. Christians, at their best, are potent revolutionaries following in the footsteps of their founder.

The five Cuban refugees we were resettling caused an immediate media storm that descended upon us unrelentingly. There were television interviews, radio interviews, press interviews and, because everyone was so tired, talks with God, asking Him to make it all stop. The Cubans, although visibly exhausted, remained incredibly polite throughout. They were in the United States, a place they equated with freedom, but weren't sure yet exactly what that meant. They hoped it meant the opportunity to work and the freedom to speak openly, without repression, as long and as loud as they wished.

The media was most interested in how these men managed to leave Cuba. One had been fortunate enough to win a visa in the lottery arrangement that has been established between Cuba and the United States. Two others fled by boat. One was on a raft at sea with ten other people for twenty hours before being picked up by the Coast Guard. The last fled by using a tire that kept his upper body above water but his legs immersed. He floated that way for a full night and day before the Coast Guard rescued him. He had been in the open ocean, completely vulnerable to whatever predator might have choosen to take his legs.

All five lived together at first, in a house we rented for this purpose. In a few months, we helped each of them find jobs and apartments. They began to send money home to relatives in Cuba. They worked on their English and on becoming consumers, American style. Before a year passed, Cuba permitted the family of the one married man in the group to join him. I was privileged to attend the party celebrating their reunion. Many felt that the impossible had occurred—it was this young husband and father we were toasting who had been afloat in a tire, praying that the sharks would overlook him.

I often recalled the risks this man took when I was tempted to play it close to the vest at the agency—for instance, when I considered saving money to balance the agency's budget rather than using it to help people in crisis. Christians are often challenged to do the opposite of what is logical or safe. We have to forget our budgets, jump in a tire, and take to the sea. We have to act more like the apostles and first converts did—a group of people who were considered by the establishment of their time as genuinely crazy, extremely dangerous, intoxicatingly happy, and strangely free.

There are things in life we will never have, no matter how we long for them. There are things we can never undo, no matter how we long to.

I have worked with people afflicted with Alzheimer's and watched them agonize trying to remember facts and events that were once at their fingertips. Very often, they can't remember and won't, and this pains them profoundly.

There are love relationships that will not be, despite all a person gives of themselves to the man or woman they love. Few things are as baffling or emotionally traumatic as unrequited love. It turns some people away from love forever.

I know physically marred people whose limbs will never be restored. They tell me they have dreams of being whole and that these dreams are so real they awaken prepared to walk, dress themselves, and go to work. Every time this happens they must reconfirm that life is not so and will never be. Each time the dream ends, they must accept it for what it was: a beautiful illusion.

Then there are the mistakes we have made, what we have said and done that we would give anything to do over and make right. I have a list of errors beyond reckoning, and everyone I know, when they face the truth, has one, too.

Pain is synonymous with Gethsemane, the garden at the foot of the Mount of Olives where Jesus took upon Himself the burden of crucifixion. His prayer here was so intense, so rending, His sweat became like drops of blood. I have been to the Mount of Olives and Gethsemane and have seen the garden where Christ went for retreat and prayer. There are eight olive trees there that some claim are three thousand years old. Others say they are surely the shoots of the trees under which Jesus prayed at the time of His sorrow, if not the originals themselves. It is one of the best places in the world I have been, although my tour permitted no more than a short visit. There is starkness and rawness in that place, and a sense of the harshness of reality in those trees that are contemporaries of Christ. The trees are beaten and weathered, but somehow still alive. When they finally succumb, they will do so with grace, having done all expected of them. They have provided shelter and fruit. They made space for His prayers and were touched by His blood.

When I left, I returned to the Gethsemanes of Paterson: to violence, to the despair of people with nothing to lose; to those seeking work or waiting for lovers or parents to return; to the ever-present back bills to pay; to some without food or a place to rest.

I must remember that God suffered at Gethsemane and that He suffers at our Gethsemanes with us. I must remember that all pain will be resolved when we return to Him. I have to accept, somehow, that we would not be free, made in His image, if the mystery of pain in this world did not exist. It seems essential to what makes us who we are, to our power to choose and transcend. Still, it is a dreadful mystery, palatable only because of His partaking of it completely.

Perhaps we are called to do what the olive trees of Gethsemane have done—to give shelter, food, and peace. To perdure despite the tragedies we witness. To live and grow though pain abides around and in us. To make a space for prayer and the answers to prayers.

Emilio was weeping when I first met him, his tears and distress causing him to look ages older than his sixty-nine years. He informed me, immediately upon shaking my hand, that he needed an attorney but could not afford one. He wanted the agency to help him secure custody of his four-year-old grandchild, Lisa Marie, before Leo, her drug-addicted father, harmed her. He kept repeating that I had to help him, and kept thanking me for my assistance, as though it had already been rendered. He said that as a fellow Italian-American, I could understand the depth of the love he had for his granddaughter and the propriety of his desire to care for her. "She is my life," he said in Italian. "You and I are the same. I know you will help me protect her from that animal."

Emilio's family history was fraught with addiction. He was a recovering alcoholic and a divorcee of nineteen years. His ex-wife, also an alcoholic, wanted nothing to do with him or her grandchild. His daughter, Lisa Marie's mother, was an active drug addict, whereabouts unknown. Lisa Marie's father, Leo, contended that he'd successfully completed two years of outpatient treatment for his drug abuse and was able to raise his daughter properly.

Leo was employed as an auto mechanic and had placed his daughter in a day care program during his working hours. He made it very clear that he gave her his full attention after work. He had cared for Lisa Marie during his addiction and through his rehabilitation. He could not fathom why his child should be taken from him now, since the period of substance abuse they weathered together was over and he was completely drug free. Emilio, however, maintained that Leo's treatment had failed and that he was still an active addict. He had refrained from bringing legal action in the past in the hope that the treatment would succeed, but it had not. Leo countered by accusing Emilio of sexually molesting Lisa Marie during a recent visit and stated he was going to court to terminate Emilio's visitation rights. Emilio replied by threatening to use the rifle he kept in his bedroom.

All of these statements were made with increasing degrees of Mediterranean emotion. Emilio's requests for help sounded more and more like demands the longer he spoke. He believed that Lisa Marie would die if not returned to him. If that happened, he would die, too, but not before killing Leo.

Eventually our staff convinced Leo to withdraw his accusation of molestation, a patent admission of its falsity. Emilio, in the end, accepted the difficulties he would encounter trying to raise a four-year-old by himself. He agreed to visitation rights of one day per week plus holidays, which sufficiently eased his concern for the care that his granddaughter was receiving. He grudgingly admitted that Leo appeared to be off drugs.

It took two months of weekly meetings and dogged negotiating by staff to finalize this relatively simple agreement. Like true Italians, Emilio and Leo frequently and unexpectedly changed their demands during this period, which made the entire process extremely frustrating. It was a gift to all of us when they finally reached consensus and ventured forth, as father and grandfather, to share responsibility for the child who needs them both.

Cases like this summon a full spectrum of emotional response and reaction from the people involved in them. There is pride, spite, vengeance, animosity, distrust, envy, and guilt on display for all to see. There can also be genuine love and concern and the sacrifice of personal self-interest in favor of the best interests of the child. God understands this kind of sacrifice and God's presence is palpable in the hearts of the people who make it. So God will be with Leo and Emilio and Lisa Marie. And Charities will be there should anything go wrong and God sends them back to us again.

Some of the boys at Mt. St. Joseph's Children's Center have been placed there by their families. Some have been abandoned by their families and placed by the state. There are usually twenty to thirty children in residence, all of them sensitive to rejection and needing to be loved.

I found out quickly that most of the boys got physical when expressing their feelings. When I would visit them, they would immediately run to me, embracing my legs and stopping me in my tracks. I would get a few light punches and arm twists as signs of affection. Because of my height they called me "Big Mike" and, despite my protestations, insisted I had been a professional basketball player. If they had seen me on the court, that illusion would have faded. In any case, they would trap me for a while and then ask the same questions they had asked the last time they captured me: Do you really run this place? (I thought so.) Do you tell the director what to do? (Sometimes.) Can I come home with you? (This destroyed me every time.) Do you get paid for coming here? (Very incisive.)

It was possible, at times, to forget that these boys were emotionally disturbed. They were all on medication, which substantially calmed them. However, there were periodic episodes of acting out—fighting, biting, and throwing things—which could occur at any time. That's why the staff and I had a minor anxiety attack when the bishop's administrative assistant called me to say he would be visiting Mt. St. Joseph's in a week to say hello to the children. I went there the very next day to say hello, again, myself.

"What's a bishop?" I was asked at least twenty times, as I talked to the children about the visit. My attempts at canonical explanation were uninteresting and my description of bishop as a spiritual father too ephemeral. When I said the bishop was my boss, however, all eyes opened. They would have to see this bishop. He must be pretty big to be Big Mike's boss. The bishop is not exceptionally tall.

The boys do not welcome every visitor to Mt. St. Joseph's with open arms. They can see right through you if you're patronizing them or using them in some way. Politicians were not permitted to visit for this reason. The boys sensed their disinterest, and reactions varied from surliness to flying fists and feet. As I said before, these are special children whose actions cannot be predicted. The bishop was definitely coming.

On the appointed day, there were twenty-four children waiting for him. Before he even said hello, he was asked, en masse, "Are you really Mike's boss?" When things quieted, the bishop avoided the question, saying his job was to make sure everyone in the diocese was loved and cared for as much as possible. This paternal response was reassuring to the children, who then felt comfortable enough to ask, "What's a diocese?" The bishop got the drift right away and realized this would go on forever unless he got the children to talk about themselves.

This is not easy for some of the boys, who are naturally protective of their self-esteem and who would, understandably, rather be silent than risk criticism. They have been laughed at and demeaned, and they don't want it to happen again. Some of the children, on the other hand, can't wait to tell you everything they have done or imagined since they've been in diapers. They crave attention and assume you are interested in all they say. They don't need you to comment, just to listen with interest. The bishop handled the situation wonderfully. He gave a big hug to each of our quiet ones and told them how beautiful and special they are to God; then he spoke with them one at a time. He quieted our talkers, after listening a bit, by doing the same thing and then by asking the boys to show him their home. With children and staff in tow, the bishop made his inspection of Mt. St. Joseph's. When he had seen the entire facility, he returned to the first floor and thanked the staff for the work they do.

While the bishop was doing this, I noticed his driver signaling to him that they must leave to stay on schedule. The bishop acknowledged the signal. I began to walk with him to his car and to thank him for coming. Some of the boys, sensing the visit was over, ran to the swings on the back lawn and pushed off. Everyone was surprised when the bishop didn't go to his car but, instead, walked over to the boys. I thought he was going to say good-bye, but he didn't. He got on a free swing and began to fly, finding a rhythm with the children to his left and right. We were all nonplused. The photographer for the diocesan newspaper, who had taken standard photos of the bishop with the children, ran to get a shot of this one—bishop on the swings. The photo appeared in the paper the following week.

The bishop was thoroughly enjoying himself, and so were the children, who had found a new compatriot. He swung hard for a good ten minutes, precious time given his duties that day. All the staff saw him and the effect, unbeknownst to him, was intensely emotional. He suddenly became a real person rather than a mysterious administrator. They could easily bond with this man of stature and responsibility, who wanted to play with the children. They loved the fact that he enjoyed the swings as much as the boys did.

A week later, when I was again at Mt. St. Joseph's, one of the boys asked, "Big Mike, when do you become a bishop?"

"I may not be ready for a long time," I said, "probably never. Is that okay?"

"Sure," he said, "let's play," which, for us, at that moment, also meant, "Let's pray." We played catch for half an hour and were both the better for it.

I started what would be a bad day, interviewing a middle-aged Hispanic mother whose adolescent daughter was pregnant for the second time. Grandma was taking care of the first child and was petrified about the possibility of extending her familial responsibilities to include the next. Mother had thrown her daughter out of the house and wanted nothing more to do with her. While trying to respect that, I said that if I could just get her signature on a document stating that her daughter was emancipated, we would be able to secure welfare payments and a small apartment for her. Incredibly, she responded, "I'll think about it." When I said, "All we need is your signature to prevent your daughter from being homeless," she started screaming at me in Spanish. She told me that she was going to sue me and, in fact, the next day she filed a complaint against me with the State Division for Youth and Family Services, the essence of which was that I tried to coerce her to help her own child. Insane as it seems, I had to discuss the complaint with a state investigator before it was dismissed. Meanwhile, we provided the young lady in distress with food, health care, counseling, and housing during and after this incident. If this angered her mother, so be it.

The State of New Jersey decided that same afternoon to inform me it had no money for salary increases for the staffs of our aging services programs. This was nonnegotiable. If the staff wanted to continue working, they would have to do so at their current salary. How to raise money to give these deserving people at least a nominal increase? The old standbys came to mind: a marathon, walkathons, dinners, dances, cake sales, bazaars, fashion shows or, perhaps, I should just put on a hair shirt and sandals and beg.

Finally, I had to terminate the employment of one of the staff—essentially for failing to consistently comply with certain regulations governing the program she worked in. She had been warned about her behavior a number of times and I knew that letting her go was the right thing to do. Still, she got very upset and that upset me.

That evening, I couldn't eat. I picked at some fruit and tried to watch television. By chance, I caught a rerun of "Adventures in

Paradise," an old series starring Gardiner McKay, who captains a sailing vessel throughout the South Pacific, encountering trouble and romance on a weekly basis. The sheer fabrication of it all put me to sleep. The next morning, I sailed to the agency—just another crewman, prone to mistakes, still learning to navigate, hoping to find his way home.

Part Three

The Recesses of the North
(Psalm 48)

Earl, one of our best volunteers, had passed away. He died overnight in the one-room apartment he'd occupied for a dozen years. The maintenance man who found him called us, reasoning we were closer to Earl than anyone else. This was true. The man had become one of us, and we took responsibility for him as quickly and solicitously as we could.

Earl's body had to be taken to the coroner's office to establish the cause of death. We all knew that whatever immediate cause was declared, it would somehow be alcohol related. He had been an astounding drinker who'd begun recovery two years ago in a final effort to give meaning to a life he felt would otherwise end without dignity. Volunteering in the agency's food pantry while struggling with his alcoholism was his way of becoming a man again. He loved working with us, loved personally helping people. He told me once over coffee that, to a small degree, it made up for letting his wife and son down during the years he was drinking.

All attempts to involve the remnants of Earl's family in his funeral failed. Either we could not locate them or the few we found refused. An elderly aunt of his said all he was good for was drinking tremendous quantities of beer. She was told that was not the Earl we knew. Because he had served in Vietnam, Earl was entitled to a veteran's funeral. One of our staff took it upon himself to make sure this happened.

When the mood was upon him, Earl would enjoy talking about religion. He was a proclaimed agnostic who, in his heart, hoped there is a God. There was the problem, however, of all his sins. He was a man of justice and felt that his many transgressions would have to be expiated before God could accept him. He was afraid of that, and consequently afraid of God. No matter how many times I assured him that God loved and forgave him, Earl held on to the residual guilt he had about his alcoholism and its effects on his family. He was an expert at condemning himself, forcing himself to atone for what he had done over and over again. There were moments when he understood he had paid his dues and that his alcoholism was a disease that, with help, he was living with successfully. He was proud of this and rightfully so. These moments were coming with greater frequency and intensity so that before his death, he was beginning to grasp he was forgiven and free to stop punishing himself.

Earl had survived most of his family. He would occasionally ask me, as if asking the universe, why his clean-living relatives were dead while a troublesome alcoholic like himself was still alive. I would tell him God is less concerned with when we die than with loving us all the time. Now that Earl is gone, I expect he has found that to be true. The Earl that I knew, the friend who pulled himself together enough to be able to help others, is learning about love from the God he had feared. Devoid of all distraction, one with the relentless compassion of God, the only concern he could possibly have is whether we are learning, too.

Thanksgiving Day had past, and with the fading light, dark feelings and black thoughts surfaced. One man wanted to kill himself because his wife had left him. Another wanted to kill the man his wife left with. A daughter would like to seriously injure the father who ignored her. All these events occurred years ago, but were resurrected with the onset of early night; fresh wounds, fresh pain.

Every year, deep autumn and winter bring an increase of people mourning their losses, mourning exacerbated by the shortening days. It is always a good time for psychiatrists and liquor store owners who prepare themselves, annually, for the suffering season.

Rita, a friend of a friend of mine, spends all winter mourning lost opportunities and her empty life. An articulate woman in her thirties, she lived at home with her parents, under the omnipresent guidance of a powerful mother. A college graduate with an English degree, she worked as an administrative assistant in a large business firm. Without a graduate degree, she was unable to find the teaching job she always wanted. She saw herself as a "typist with a title," and said that she was dead-ended professionally. She didn't date, mother having effectively discouraged the men who were interested in her. Only a doctor or lawyer would satisfy mother, which limited the dating pool considerably. Rita worked, ate, slept, shopped for clothes, occasionally went to the movies, and got depressed around this time of year.

Once, when I suggested she do some volunteer work, perhaps help out at the agency during Christmas, she actually said she didn't have the time. What she meant was she didn't have time for anyone but herself. She enjoyed dwelling on her problems, had no intention of ever confronting her mother, and relished a few months of therapy each year, where she was the center of attention. Anyway, she knew she would feel better come spring and then wouldn't need Prozac or therapy for a while. I left open the invitation to volunteer, hoping it would be helpful to her year round to begin thinking about someone other than herself.

Porfirio was a victim of lost love. He had been severely depressed since his lover left him, and thought about nothing but why it happened and how to get her back. He had sent her letters and gifts to no avail. She refused to see him and did not return his phone calls. After work, Porfirio stayed home alone, drinking, considering the futility of his life and the reasons why he was a failure. He had a good job and an admirable home, but those meant nothing; he wanted someone to share his life with, to marry and have children with, and he wanted this with the woman who had rejected him.

A week before Christmas, Porfirio started talking vaguely about suicide. Because any allusion to suicide is serious, psychotherapy was arranged for him immediately. He would receive therapy as frequently as needed and was given an emergency telephone number that would enable him to get help twenty-four hours a day.

Winter wore on and no one, thank God, killed themselves or anyone else. Porfirio was in therapy and reportedly doing well. Rita surprised me by collecting canned goods for our food pantry. She said she felt less depressed after doing this and was willing to try it again. The staff set up a birdfeeder that drew robins and chickadees, sparrows and doves—each especially beautiful in the crisp air and snow. All things considered, the season had been good.

Four years ago, my relationship with a truly remarkable woman ended. There are many reasons why our life together crashed and burned, all of them valid enough to substantiate annulment. There are some things people just cannot abide even after twelve years of trying. Nevertheless, the parting was painful for us both. We had experienced times of memorable joy and of heartfelt sharing. There were times of great anger, however, that damaged our psyches and our souls, and a formidable intransigence, on both our parts, that never lessened. These we could not overcome without changing into people we did not wish to be.

When I approached life as a single man once more, I felt injured, empty, and profoundly lost. Later, day by day, I realized I was incredibly free. The house in the suburbs, and its attendant cares, was gone. The neighbors who never understood what I said about the poor were now miles away. My Petrine personality could again express itself without being criticized by suburbanites who admittedly avoided the world of the underprivileged.

Understand I have no problem with families living in beautiful homes, enjoying what our society can provide to those who are affluent. I do have a problem, however, with people who refuse to acknowledge that others live in debilitating, degrading conditions and need help. I have a definitive parting of the way with the affluent people I know who care little or nothing about the poor and excuse their behavior by saying the needy should help themselves. People who put five dollars or less in the collection basket on Sunday and believe this discharges their responsibility to the homeless, the jobless, and the ill do not amuse me. That's my Petrine personality. Saint Peter got into serious trouble for vociferously speaking his mind and for his willingness to take action. Sometimes, trouble is our best alternative.

Driving to work one morning, I saw a man pick a beer bottle out of someone's garbage and put it to his mouth for a possible sip. This is the reality of Paterson. You can either do something to alleviate the pain here or continue driving and, at night, after dinner and television, forget what you saw and seek the solace of sleep. You must decide what that man means to you. He is important or he is nothing. If he is important, some action on your part must follow.

I have accepted that a long relationship is over, and that this is best for both of us. She required I become a different me, a non-Petrine person. I wonder if it's possible, after all these years, for me to change, or if it's even sound for me to try. I cannot, in my stomach, abide mowing the lawn and then discussing it for the rest of the day. I cannot listen to endless speeches about unexpected bargains discovered amidst angry seas of shoppers. I disdain, with fervor, being forced to hear about someone's important connections, cultivated over decades for some obtuse desire. I am troubled because in the midst of this, people are going without food and there are people without heat when the cold comes. I am utterly dismayed by my former neighbors' ability to ignore these realities.

I can be a hard person to live with because of what I think and say. I've been a hard person to live with because of things I've done. Still, there is something so repulsive to me about living vacuously that I willingly become Petrine whenever the threat of that occurs. Lord Jesus Christ, have mercy on me, a sinner.

One Paterson evening, during the hellish winter of 1996, I asked a man who was walking up and down Cianci Street, talking to himself, if he needed help. His face was dirty, his hair was wild, and he wasn't walking well. He might have been drunk or just coming off a binge. He might just have been beaten up by the weather. I remember asking him to come inside the agency, warm up, wash, and get something to eat. He looked to be in his late forties, a white man, six foot one or two, and thinner than he had any right to be. I could tell how tall he was because as soon as I stopped speaking he was in my face, yelling at the top of his voice for me to leave him alone. Instinctively, I got my hands up because I thought he was going to throw a punch. Instead, he ambled away, cursing mightily, calling down the wrath of God on Western civilization and, presumably, on me in particular. Nothing was accomplished here but my disturbing a poor man's reveries. When I went to work the next morning, the day's problems put this incident out of mind.

A week later, it was nine degrees and snowing. The same man was in our clothes room, trying on gloves and boots that had been donated to us. When he noticed me, he said, "Thanks for letting me pick my own stuff." It was the last thing I expected to hear and it was a pleasure to ask him to take his time and make sure he got what he needed. When he finished, he apologized for his behavior at our first meeting. I told him the truth, that it was forgotten as far as I was concerned. Of greater importance now was whether we could offer him any other help to get through the winter. He said, "No, I'm leaving Paterson as soon as I can. It's too cold here. I'm going to hitch rides for a while until I find a place I like." With that, we shook hands and he began his journey.

At times I admit I was envious of this man. He had the freedom and lack of attachments I sometimes desperately craved. Imagine being able to say you are going to travel around until you find a place that you like. Imagine being able to seek the warmth, the sky, and the people that please you. In any case, he was gone and I remained in Paterson. The Paterson of ancient streets and crumbling concrete, of dilapidated buildings and broken people.

The Paterson that embraces misery in all its fascinating forms—alcoholism, drug addictions, malnutrition, exposure, violence, and wanton self-destruction.

At sunset, when the weather is obliging, the sky above Paterson is almost beautiful and the light falling on the steeple of the Cathedral of St. John the Baptist truly is. I could see that light from my office, and often wished I could capture it for the entire city to bathe in. People in Paterson need jobs and food, shelter, clothing, and self-respect. For reasons as personal as their souls, they do not migrate to sun and warmth but continue to struggle and reside there. That being the case, they need this light to remind themselves that they are beautiful, that their children are beautiful, and that life can be saner and less destructive than they know. Part of my work was to point out this light, whenever I was able.

I had just been told, by a woman who knew me very well, that I'd lost my sense of fun. This came after I peremptorily escaped from a cocktail party during which I had to say, to what seemed an endless array of people, how wonderful it was to learn that their careers were so successful, their homes so unique, their gardens so lovely, and their children so comely and intelligent. All of this was done within earshot of other people I had similarly praised. No problem. Everyone was satisfied, never questioning for a moment how strange it was that they all simultaneously enjoyed the attributes and qualities I was attesting to. When the conversation turned to reducing Medicaid expenditures for the poor, however, and I realized I was alone in opposing this, I left, citing work-related exhaustion. If I hadn't, I might have ignited a verbal war with one hard-liner or another that would have achieved absolutely nothing. I have finally learned that it's impossible to convince some people to change their opinions in the presence of others. Any attempt to do so constitutes a major threat to their egos which, perforce, they furiously defend.

Nonetheless, the next morning I was told that I'd lost my sense of fun. The party was still reverberating in my critic's head as she expressed her abhorrence over the opportunity I'd wasted to learn about the lives of so many interesting people. I suggested, a bit defensively, that after Sunday Mass we go hiking, or at least walking, in a nearby state park. That, I said with overt sarcasm, might be fun. We went, and I definitely did enjoy the outing. Back home, with lungs and legs in working order once more, I felt compelled to examine this issue of fun, wondering just how much of an old crank I had become.

There is no doubt that many of the pursuits I had a rabid interest in years ago seem insignificant to me now—baseball, football, deep sea fishing, and modern art are just a few salient examples. My youthful desire to become a great writer has given way to concern for my son's and daughter's well-being, dedication to my work, and the happiness received from reading, prayer, and listening to the life stories of people willing to honestly share their experiences. I always find these stories important. All of our lives have episodes replete with beauty, strength, and holiness that are honored in the telling.

Most people need to find or create substantive meaning in life, to find or create integrity and value. Regardless of their income, their level of education, or their disabilities, people want, somehow, to live meaningfully. It makes no difference if they are taxi drivers, university professors, or inner-city gang members. For the affluent, this need is often satisfied through acquisition. In time, having purchased the houses and cars they desired, the sound systems and swimming pools, they find themselves without goals other than purchasing newer or bigger models of what they already have. If they sense a dearth of meaning in their lives, it's because they've distanced themselves from the needs and problems of others. They have lost touch with the holiness of sharing and helping—a holiness that clothes, cars, and computers cannot provide.

I have seen the homeless give gloves and hats to other street people during terrible winters. I have watched developmentally disabled people put themselves out to make life easier for the roommates in their group home. I have been taken by the solicitude of an emotionally disturbed child, gently comforting another child who is acting out, trying to make him understand that life has not ended because of some small disappointment. These people, despite their station in life, are often more caring than my neighbors and fellow parishioners, who erect boundaries around themselves that denote exactly how much assistance, both personal and monetary, they will give others. Our society will remain essentially insensitive until such time as our attitudes toward self-aggrandizement and self-denial change. Some fun will have to be offered up; some leisure sacrificed. Christ's vision of love and compassion must become the reality we work to achieve. This may not be fun, but it is genuine and authentic, meaningful and holy.

I have a friend, an artist who, during his apprenticeship, visited all the important museums in the United States and Europe. He told me, once, that in Madrid he gave a cap he needed to a man who needed it more. He remembers this incident with greater clarity than any of the paintings he saw in the Prado. He believes that this gratuitous act of giving, and others like it in his life, are the most important things he's done. He understands these acts to be his best art because each of them is the medium through which he has created the person he has become. He is not a proud man; he knows his deficiencies. He also knows he can do much good in little ways and is alert for opportunities to serve. From our many conversations, I can testify that he thoroughly enjoys his life and work. He has experienced more and had more fun than a dozen other people I know. But he will tell you, if asked, that his life is meaningful because of what he has given of himself.

The woman who counseled me to have more fun was a very determined person. She kept at me about this until, out of desperation, and in a moment of evident madness, I agreed to go cross-country skiing with her. It was easy, she said. Anyone could do it. It would benefit me, physically and mentally. I should take her word for it—I would love it.

I went. I tried. I fell. It is possible that I have the worst coordination on snow and ice of anyone who ever tried this sport.

In an effort to encourage me, my friend gave me my own set of skis as a special gift. This meant, of course, that I must try to learn to use them. I did, and fell with even greater frequency than before. The scenery, at least, was beautiful, even though I saw it from various sprawled positions and actually became a part of it every minute or so.

There was no third attempt. I went back to Paterson and back to work: places fraught with problems and dangers of their own, but where, as best I can recall, I'd never needed help to stand and I'd never fallen down. I enjoyed remaining upright. It was fun.

Men and women I know who work in the helping professions have told me of suffering periodic bouts of what the monks of antiquity called *acedia*. This is a psychological state of listlessness and depression during which the measure of one's abilities, one's efforts to help others, and one's very value as a person are questioned. I have suffered it myself and can attest to the disorientation and isolation it engenders. It is a time when meaninglessness prevails, when your past seems a total mistake, and any goals you may have appear empty and vacuous. Nothing is pleasant; everything is stale.

I have a friend who has steadfastly avoided this condition despite working for over fourteen years with destitute immigrants settling in Paterson. She gives herself completely to her work, devoting her evenings and weekends, when necessary, to the people in her care. She has made what monks call a conversion of manners that requires her to give herself wholly to others, seek no recognition for her efforts, and live a life of great simplicity. She is held in respect by all who work with her and is a model many emulate, to everyone's benefit. She is not a saint by any means. Just a woman attempting to live as she believes Christ would have her.

My acedia heals when I accept my fallibility and acknowledge that God loves me, faults and all. It returns when I forget this and insist on having to be perfect in order to earn God's love. The willful desire to attain perfection is an expression of personal pride that says, in effect, I can attain salvation alone. My constant failure to achieve this brings on the inevitable acedia that attempts to convince me of my worthlessness. The question that leads to acedia is: Shall I insist on demanding more of myself than God does?

Thomas Merton relates a devastating Zen tale that is applicable here. Upon reaching a stream, two monks were approached by a woman of great beauty, who asked them to help her across. Out of charity, one of them took her on his back, carried her across, and put her down on dry ground. Some ten miles down the road, his companion began to berate him for breaking the rule forbidding monks to touch or have any close contact with a woman. The accused monk walked along silently, but then remarked, with the gentlest of smiles, "I released the weight of that woman upon crossing the stream, but you have been carrying her now for ten miles more."[2]

It was not yet Christmas and already our resources were being strained by people without heat, proper clothing, and food. Carlos, an unemployed single parent, was so excited about our paying a small gas bill for him that he forgot to take the food he also needed. He returned the next morning, hungry and embarrassed. He took two bags of groceries for himself and his son, which would probably hold him until his food stamp approval came through. If he needed more, he knew he could come back to us. The security this gave him was almost as important as the food he left with.

Rudy, a middle-aged black man, was sobbing in the waiting room. He lived in a welfare hotel and, while he was out begging breakfast, his room was broken into. All his belongings, his clothes, hot plate, and radio were stolen. He had nothing left but what he was wearing, not even a working lock on his door. I spoke to him for over an hour trying to reassure him. We found him clothes from our stock, gave him canned food and some spending money, and talked to his hotel manager who was willing to replace the lock right away. There was a hot plate that had been donated to us that he could have. This man had spent time in prison for possession of narcotics and six months in a drug rehab program. Cocaine was his drug of choice and he told me how stupid he had been to sacrifice so much for the few minutes of pleasure crack cocaine brought. He said he would take any job he could get but mentioned, as an aside, that he was a trained welder. When I jumped on this, he was genuinely surprised. He didn't think he could ever get a high-paying job again after his troubles.

One of our social workers, Curtis, somehow learned of every job opening in the area. When I referred Rudy to him, he was delighted to find his new client had a trade. He knew employers who needed skilled craftsmen and guaranteed he would have Rudy working in a week or two at most. Curtis would buy Rudy work clothes with agency funds and would be ready, when Rudy had worked a bit, to help him find an apartment he could afford.

Rudy already had another goal that he was very serious about. He wanted to buy a car, any kind of car, just as long as it would get him to Virginia and back. His wife, who left him during his active addiction, had moved to Norfolk and he wanted to see her. He wanted to drive up to her home in his own car, healthy, in new clothes, with money in his pockets. He had never stopped loving her. He wanted to take her out to dinner and talk about everything that had happened to them. "Even if she never takes me back," he said, "I want her to know I'm sorry for what I did and that I'm okay." Rudy planned to do this after a full year of work, when he was fit and feeling good about himself. One thing at a time, I thought to myself. I'd seen too many dreams dissolve in a lot less than a year's time.

Before he left with Curtis, Rudy wished me a holy Christmas. Not a merry Christmas or a happy Christmas, but a holy Christmas. I wished him holiness, too, and the peace that passes understanding.

A Hispanic woman who had come to us for counseling on and off during the year stopped by to say hello. She was very intelligent, very personable, and very unsure of herself. Her mother, for reasons of her own, had decided to dedicate her life to criticizing everything this woman did. She never knew her father and had no one to help her ward off her mother's barrage. For her own protection, she had taken low-risk jobs with few responsibilities in order to avoid any possibility of failure. She worked as a secretary to support two children and a husband who was rarely employed. He found the jobs available to him beneath his dignity, but did not allow his pride to keep him from living off her income, spending it as he saw fit. The thought of losing him petrified her, even though she suspected him of sleeping with other women. She would not risk confronting him about anything and never went further than occasionally complaining to friends about his behavior. She needed him to satiate her low self-esteem, to show that, at least, she had a husband—his deficiencies notwithstanding. She talked about the gifts she would surprise her magnificent spouse with on Christmas morning. Of course, that he would give her anything was doubtful. After all, he was unemployed. I listened politely, knowing she deserved better and wondering how she could be so happy.

These tales of difficult and damaged love were becoming ever more common among the people we served. In fact, they had become the norm rather than the exception. Hearing them made me realize how fortunate I was to witness and receive so much real love in my life.

I had the constant love of family and close friends and the love of so many of the broken people I knew: the addicted, homeless, lonely, and ill people who knew I was broken by weaknesses and illness too. And there was the love expressed by hundreds of people in the community, who made time in their lives to help the poor. During the first days of winter that year, cars and station wagons full of food and clothing arrived, donated from parishes throughout the diocese. It was enough to keep us going for weeks.

I tried to express my appreciation in thank-you letters sent to the parishes, but couldn't convey what I really wanted to say. I wanted to express the thanks the poor themselves would give through hugs and tears and handshakes and bless-yous. Simple gestures and simple words that mean they would do the same for you should you ever be in trouble. I wanted to say, too, that it is beautiful to believe that this is true.

A series of unavoidable expenditures descended upon us one year, mostly related to building repairs and heating system upgrades that should have been attended to before, but weren't for lack of money. The result was that we couldn't formulate a balanced budget for the upcoming fiscal year without limiting salary increases for staff to two percent of their present wage. It was a small amount, given the rising cost of living, but it was all that was possible. I could get no more assistance from the Chancery, other than what was needed to cover that two percent, and so it had to be.

I had a morning meeting with the program directors who were affected, and gave them the bad news. It would be their job to convey it to their staff. The directors responded stoically, without fuss or complaint. God knows none of us were in it for money, but there are always considerations, like food and housing costs, that must be addressed. I promised, on my word, that I would try my best to do better for them the following year, and I know they believed me. Their trust was the only consolation I took from the whole affair.

That same afternoon, I was told that we had not sold enough tickets to a fashion show fund-raiser to make the revenue it would generate worthwhile. I would have to spend hours hawking the event, calling old supporters and new acquaintances, talking, then pleading, for their participation. The money raised would be used by our emergency assistance programs, which were always in need of funds. It somehow seemed incongruous to me to ask women to admire lavish fashions for the benefit of people in worn clothes. I often thought how much more fruitful it would be if those who attend would simply donate the price of their tickets without demanding a show. But that will never happen.

To complete the day, a van used by one of the drug rehab centers the agency operates, a vehicle admittedly from the Pleistocene, finally died. It was beyond repair and had to be replaced post-haste. There was no money in the budget for this, but what choice did I have? I gave my consent to purchase another with a short remonstration to the center's manager that she be thrifty for the sake of us all. By that time our comptroller had a headache that defied aspirin and was trying, successfully, to pass it on to me.

That night, I decided to work late so I could worry about deficits and expenditures awhile longer in private. Within an hour, someone was ringing the entrance bell at the front door, then knocking and ringing again. I hurried downstairs, fumbled over the many locks the neighborhood made necessary, and admitted a tiny woman of great age into the building. She told me she'd seen my office light on and thought she would try her luck. She was living on Social Security and could not make ends meet. That month she had used almost all her money for rent and utilities and didn't have enough for food. She said she would keep her gas and electric bills down to the minimum so that this never happened again and mentioned, in self-defense, that she didn't have a telephone. She filled two grocery bags with items from the food pantry and took ten dollars for milk and meats she would need while waiting for her next check. I offered her twenty, but she absolutely wouldn't take that much. When she left, she blessed me—a blessing as meaningful as any I've received from priests or bishops.

Driving home, I thought that helping this woman, and others like her, was the best use we could make of the money we had. The fiscal problems I'd worried about all day were important, but not as critical as meeting the immediate, personal needs of people. This is the purpose of Catholic Charities and always will be. Reminding me of this was the second blessing she gave me that evening.

Martin told me what follows on an August afternoon—an afternoon when I had many things to do, none of which were more important to me than listening to his story. He was a big man, just past fifty, who was interested in serving as a volunteer and wanted to know if that was possible. The first thing he told me was that he was an alcoholic and heroin addict, six years into recovery.

"I lost everything I could think of and still didn't want to recover. I lost my wife, my daughter, my parents, my friends, my job, my home, my car, my clothes, my self-respect. It began to mean nothing to lose my life too. I only entered rehab to avoid jail, after I was busted for disorderly conduct and possession. The jails were full or I wouldn't have been offered an alternative. I'm not sure I can do time and never want to find out if I can.

"I hated the rehab program until I realized I actually could recover and really had only one choice—to do it or give up living. I probably was healed because the people running the program insisted on it. They refused to consider failure as a possibility. I love those people for sticking with me, even though I said some terrible things to them at times. It took a long while, over a year, to become comfortable with everything again. I found that the key for me is simplicity, to simplify things and appreciate—appreciate myself and the good things around me.

"I was lucky to find a job and a small apartment. I got work as a custodian—handyman is more like it—in a building complex in Paterson. My living quarters are there, rent free, as part of my pay. I have a cat and I read a lot. I still get depressed sometimes and angry with myself for what I did, but less than I used to.

"Mostly, though, I'm not afraid of much anymore. I've failed, so I'm not afraid of failure. I'm poor and tired, but free. Does that make sense to you? When I see people worrying about their careers and their futures and how much they need, I'm glad that's not me. People are anxious and preoccupied, always planning and conniving. I was like that once, but I'm not now and don't ever have to be again.

"I do have some plans, though. I save a little money when I can because, if I live long enough, I want to retire. I'm going to buy property in New York, around Kingston, and have a cabin built on it where I can live. I like that area a lot. There are still woods there, and that's where I'll build. I want to be quiet and enjoy the woods. But while I'm here, working, I'd like to be of help to people. So, that's another plan—to be a volunteer and do some good."

There was never a time the agency didn't need help, so it was easy to suggest ways Martin could serve as a volunteer. He decided to begin by accompanying the staff on visits to homebound people. He helped clean these people's residences, did their laundry, went grocery shopping for them, and just stayed with them for a while to talk about whatever they wished. He was very good at all of this and soon had more requests for his services than he could handle.

As for Martin's future plan, I confess it seemed more like a fantasy to me. But it was a fantasy I wanted to believe in. It would be wonderful to visit Martin's cabin and share in the peace he created there. I'd been to Kingston and knew the stillness of its woods. It's a great place to be free.

Irene's eyes captured me the moment I met her. They were almost always sad, even when she smiled. Years later, old and alone, riddled with cancer, and dying much too slowly for her taste, her eyes stayed sad throughout the day.

Our first meeting was autumns ago, at a parish where she had enthusiastically volunteered to organize a clothing drive for the poor, and where I had gone to speak in support of her effort. Since that time, she had never stopped collecting clothing for us to distribute. It became a personal project for her that she worked at year-round, until she grew too ill to continue.

When I saw her last, hospitalized for yet another time, she told me to give her entire wardrobe away. I was to do the same with her furniture and anything else of use she owned. She had made provision for this in her will. She asked me to promise her that she would be buried quickly—no viewing, she didn't want that. Just Mass and burial without fuss of any sort. I gave her my word it would be as she wished. She wasn't expected to live another month; she felt death coming that very week. Her heart failed before five days passed.

Irene didn't see herself as special or unusual in any way, although she was to me and to a great many others as well. Her generosity had become natural, as much a part of her as her walk and manner of speech. She made little of it, because giving of herself was simply the right thing to do. She found that she could be of help and tried to be. Enough said.

Buddhists speak of people who are old souls, people who have been born many times and who have accrued great wisdom, which comes to bear in their present incarnation. I do not ascribe to reincarnation, but the concept "old soul" seems applicable, allegorically, to some women and men I have met. They are always unobtrusive, centered, available to others, quietly committed to addressing the misery they find in the world, and empathetic to a degree few understand. Irene was such a soul, and it brought abiding sadness to her eyes.

Once, Irene and I talked about the frailty of our bodies as she prepared to undergo another round of endless medical exams. She didn't complain about the testing and probing that again awaited her. "After a while," she said, "you realize that you can't control things. You give up trying to manage and direct what happens, and concentrate on the good people who are around you. I've met some wonderful people at the hospital." Another time, she told me her body had become a hindrance, and that she had begun the process of letting go of it.

Irene had vivid recollections of her family's country home, of shrines and cathedrals she had visited, and of quiet, secret places she had found and made her own. She considered her most important relationships and was, on the whole, satisfied with them all. There had been conflicts and problems, of course, but God understood these things and knew she regretted any sorrow she had caused. She was ready for death when it came.

Before this happened, she created a riddle, a Zen koan really, for both of us to ponder: What will the world be like without Irene? Her response: "As it was before she was born." Mine: "As it is with the love she's given." Irene laughed and admitted she liked my answer better.

For almost a year, I had been involved in negotiations with representatives of a private nonprofit agency in Passaic, trying to achieve the mutually desired goal of their joining the diocese. This agency was, for all intents and purposes, Catholic, being founded and led by a Catholic administrator, with a Catholic board of directors and a mission of service to the poor identical to Catholic Charities. The diocesan hierarchy had good reason for giving me permission to explore the union. Passaic, the second largest city in the Diocese of Paterson, was without any significant church-sponsored social services. Service programs were definitely needed there and one of my priorities had been to develop them. Being able to work with this agency, as a new part of Catholic Charities, would open the door to a variety of opportunities to do exactly that.

It took months of phone calls and meetings to resolve everyone's concerns, which ranged from employee benefits issues and changes in personnel policies, to board responsibilities and long-range planning under diocesan auspices. When final agreement was reached, I asked the bishop's secretary to help us schedule a reception at which he would formally welcome the Passaic agency into the diocese. It was at this point that the entire effort had to be abandoned.

I was telephoned by the Chancellor and told that, upon the advice of the diocesan fiscal office, the proposed union had been rejected. I was not told who made the final decision on this, although I inquired. The reason given was a small deficit in the Passaic organization's operating budget and the fear that this might increase in the future. The diocese did not want to have to allocate any of its funds to help, should that be the case. I was not allowed to contest the decision. I did say it seemed remarkably precipitous given the fact that the deficit in question was not large and that I had a history, well known to the Chancery, of balancing budgets. I was told that "unfortunately" the decision was final.

It was left to me to convey this decision to the Passaic group—an unenviable task, at best. I understood the Chancery's position, but regarded it as dangerously shortsighted. When I presented it, those who had opposed becoming part of the diocese would feel justified. They would say they had known all along that they couldn't count on the Church. The others, who'd supported the plan, would be terribly disappointed and might well be angry with me and the system I represented. I would have to explain the diocese's position as best I could but would not concur with it. As I saw it, a fertile opportunity to help people was being lost for fear of the minimal risk involved.

When I went to Passaic and related all that had happened, there was bitterness and anger, but also, to my surprise, a continued desire among many present to work cooperatively with Catholic Charities. After some very healthy venting, we decided to move ahead by ourselves. We agreed to share our food and clothing resources and our vans and drivers, as needed. When feasible, we would also submit letters of support for each other's funding requests and program proposals. In effect, because our missions were identical, we chose to operate as church—unofficially, but church nonetheless.

Someone said the whole situation reminded her of parts of the Acts of the Apostles that describe how the various communities of the new faith struggled with internal problems and external difficulties. Others agreed that the comparison was appropriate; we were all trying to be people of faith and people of church. At meeting's end, we prayed to become so, regardless of names, labels, budgets, and bills.

If you think the Pharisees have vanished in time, you are very mistaken. My mother was once soundly berated by a Pharisee friend for not visiting the family gravesite one holiday and placing flowers in the appropriate, God-designated places. This omission, said the Pharisee, was sinful and not to be excused by other personal or familial obligations. Neither was it exonerated by my mother's donation of food that holiday to Catholic Charities. No! Graves must be visited and flowers placed, without fail.

To make matters worse, the Pharisee in question was a famous hoarder and notorious racist. His excuse for not contributing more than he did to the Church was that any extra money received would be used to help lazy, minority people who should be forced to help themselves. This he would not give for, but he would spend money decorating graves and speak proudly of it.

There are Pharisees among the clergy, their vociferous denial of allegiance to this sect not withstanding. These people spend more time choosing the proper vestments and creating beautiful liturgies than they do on the meaning of the liturgies they lead. They dedicate more energy to ritual than to meaning, which is why many of their parishioners take little home with them after Mass, other than the sense of an obligation fulfilled.

There are Pharisees within the nonprofit world: administrators who relish the prestige and perks of their position; who accept cars, expense accounts, and opportunities to travel; and who seek a place of honor at banquets and ceremonies. They enjoy their authority and the respect accorded them. Although they see themselves as representing the disenfranchised people their agencies serve, many of them haven't had meaningful contact or dialogue with a poor person in years.

We are probably all pharisaical to some degree. I showed my fidelity to this timeless sect whenever I put paperwork before people or budget-balancing before community needs. I was pharisaical whenever I was overly concerned with the media, with my public image and the image of Catholic Charities.

It isn't easy to resign from the Pharisees. It requires effort to free ourselves from their beliefs and attitudes, from their posturing and sense of self-satisfaction. The reward for those who try, however, is to live and grow as Christians.

My affinity for "pharisaism" found expression in other ways as well. Over the years, it had been my privilege to receive a number of plaques and awards that, along with my academic degrees, were prominently displayed on the walls of my office. I took great comfort in this display. Like a true Pharisee, I found satisfaction in these signs of recognition, and believed they genuinely reflected my value as a person.

At one with this desire for recognition and affirmation was a longing for certainty and control. The Pharisees thought they could guarantee salvation through the proper and correct application of ritual. I sought a similar guarantee by seeking unassailable truth in philosophy and religion. I wanted all the answers at my fingertips so that I should suffer no anxiety and would always know exactly what to do to be saved. The writer Richard Bode calls this "dogma sickness,"[3] and for a time I was immensely ill with it.

It took a near fatal bout of viral encephalitis to make me realize how pharisaical I'd become. It required catastrophic illness and a long, painful recovery for me to understand that God's love was not conditioned upon what I achieved. What I saw during recovery was how pitiful, unnecessary, and untoward my attempts to prove my self-worth really were, how immature I was to believe my value increased with the recognition I received. I was setting myself apart from others, proclaiming with every new award that I was gifted, better, special. When disease reduced me to nothing, totally dependent on the care of nurses and therapists, all this was revealed for what it was—resoundingly false. I was just one more person in the hospital, one more case in rehab, who was treated, thank God, exactly the same as everyone else. Divested of everything I relied upon as proof of my stature, I found that the Creator of the universe was not impressed by any of my achievements. Instead, I felt He was more than happy with the "me" that was left after all the baggage I carried was gone.

An elderly woman suffering from Parkinson's disease came to my office demanding to see me. She was very upset and quite insistent. I saw her as soon as I could, fully prepared to offer any assistance Charities could provide. Actually, she didn't need any help herself. She had just read an article about Mother Teresa of Calcutta, was suitably impressed by it, and felt that Catholic Charities should more closely emulate Mother Teresa's efforts. Specifically, she felt that Charities should do more to help the homeless. The way she said this made it clear she was both expressing an opinion and laying down a challenge. We spoke for quite a while and I agreed with much of what she said. There was always more that we could do, not only for the homeless, but for everyone in need. Her challenge was a worthwhile goal for an old Pharisee like myself to strive for, as long as I remembered, every inch of the way, to try to strive for it selflessly. It was time to begin to bare my walls.

After the day's work was done, I often lingered for some minutes at the entrance to the agency. Regardless of the season, people would be out on the streets. After I locked up and went home, there would be drugs sold and used on those streets. There would be drinking, prostitution, fighting, and theft. Some people would return home from work to loved ones and friends. Others would spend the night alone. Some would sleep in peace while others wished they could. Many would thank God for another day. Some would consider the entire day an experience worth missing.

One evening, I lingered longer than usual. Henri Nouwen had died that day, a passing that was a great loss for us all. I do not exaggerate when I say that this man's writings will ennoble and heal you. Nowhere have I found the truth of God's unconditional love expressed more clearly than in his books. From his heart, he declared, again and again, what we should already know from the Gospels but find so hard to believe: that God is love and love only; that our fear, alienation, and despair come from the world and ourselves, not God; that God wants to love, and does love, without limits; that whatever we have done that shames us is forgiven before we ask. This is the "good news" of Christianity that Nouwen never tired of telling.

Henri Nouwen's search for authenticity and meaning, as a Christian in the world, led him to simplify his life. After twenty years as a teacher of pastoral psychology, pastoral theology, and spirituality, after achieving renown as an author and lecturer, he found himself in crisis. Unfulfilled by his work, unable to pray well, and becoming estranged from other people, he resigned his teaching position at Harvard University to live with and minister to mentally disabled people at Daybreak, a community residence near Toronto. At Daybreak he wasn't a famous person accorded the special treatment that comes with recognition. The residents were unable to read any of his published works and were unaware of his past accomplishments. They knew only the Henri Nouwen who was present to them, and this freedom helped Nouwen become present to himself and God. He had to face and overcome temptations to be "relevant" and "powerful" in the world's eyes in order to do this. He had to change his ministry and career in a way that many would consider self-destructive, a bad move by secular standards.

Before his death, Nouwen understood this move as one that took him forward toward his real goal: a closer, more genuine relationship with Christ. The care he gave to the disabled people he lived with made this possible. They had shown him the way toward an authentic life, and he was grateful for their help.

No one on Paterson's streets that evening had any idea who Henri Nouwen was. Having grown beyond the need for recognition, this wouldn't have bothered or surprised him in the least. He is now within the totality of love he always knew was waiting. Where we will follow in due course.

I am fascinated by a story told by Elie Wiesel in his book, *Four Hasidic Masters and Their Struggle against Melancholy*. In it, he relates the conspiratorial efforts of Reb Mendel of Riminov, the Maggid of Kozhenitz, and the Seer of Lubin to hasten the coming of the Messiah.

It was the beginning of the nineteenth century and the time seemed right, to these three masters, for the Redeemer's return. Europe was in turmoil and change throughout the Age of Enlightenment and the Napoleonic Wars. In the name of liberation, enlightenment had generated its own myths and darkness, its own prisons and persecutions. Kings lost their thrones only to be replaced by different kinds of kings. Judges became victims, and victims judges, in accord with the prevalent political scene.

The upheaval of war after war could be traced to the presence of one man: Napoleon. For Reb Medel of Riminov, Napoleon was the incarnation of the Gog of Magog, the opponent of the Messiah, who must first be victorious in order to be defeated by him. All three masters agreed that the times were apocalyptic. The bloodshed and social disorder were clear signs that the end of the world was near. Jews were suffering and dying all over Europe and needed the Messiah as never before. The masters thought, "Why wait for him when Jewish lives are being lost by the hour? Why not run to him, make him appear through our own means?" They truly believed that their prayers and deeds could influence the course of battles and wars and bring the Messiah forth. They believed this, but despite meeting after fervent meeting, after comparing notes and attempting to coordinate their plans, they failed. The reason? They could not, as Elie Wiesel states, agree on tactics. Only Reb Mendel was willing to give Napoleon unqualified support. The other two had serious doubts about the biblical and prophetic proportions of the emperor's character. As a result, Napoleon, having failed to become the Gog of Magog, was defeated, and the Messiah could not come. The Hasidim must wait for another time, for another generation that will be the blessed one.[4]

Christians have waited for the Second Coming for almost two thousand years. There have been numerous times it was thought to be near. The appearance of comets, the devastation of plagues and wars, the immanent possibility of nuclear disaster: all have been interpreted as portents of Christ's return. Still, we wait. Life and history have continued, to the dismay of those who thought the final glory was at hand. Sometimes, like the three masters, I want to hasten the Promised One along. Like them, I cannot agree on a strategy to accomplish this. I can only pray, "Thy kingdom come," and have faith that it will.

I recall a very warm Paterson summer afternoon. I helped a young woman, Angela, find the groceries she needed and clothes for her seven-year-old son, David. David started to explore the food pantry, building a structure with canned goods of all kinds. He got annoyed when we interrupted his project to have him try on shirts for size. At certain ages, of which seven is one, boys hate to try on clothing; a matter of genetic coding, possibly. When the distasteful task was done, he immediately returned to his building.

Angela didn't reveal much about her life, other than she couldn't find work and got despondent sometimes. The boy's father, as I so often heard, had left long ago for parts unknown. For a few seconds, Angela forgot her problems and smiled before she left. David followed, clutching two small cans of corn: his new and precious toys.

For those with eyes to see, the Messiah had come and gone, again.

I was far from Brooklyn and Paterson, on retreat at St. Joseph's Abbey, a Cistercian monastery in Spencer, Massachusetts. It was a pristine autumn day, the kind that tourists and photographers travel to New England for. The leaves had begun to turn and the contrast between their colors and the blue of the sky was welcome to eyes that had grown tired of cities.

That day, walking alone some distance from the abbey church, I understood God loved me. This was love that came from within and without. It was centered in me, yet transcended me. It was love so accepting and powerful that I knew my many faults were forgiven and my shortcomings forgotten. I was forgiven, cherished, valued, embraced, and relentlessly loved by God—and this all seemed incredibly natural and appropriate.

That day, I realized that as broken as we all are, we are loved. As selfish and manipulative, proud and possessive, as all of us can be, we are loved. This is the revelatory message of Christianity that so many people find impossible to accept. Nevertheless, God's unconditional love for us is what Christ taught. You can dismiss this teaching, trivialize it, or label it surreal—or you can be healed, consoled, and nurtured by it. Either way, you are loved.

As Christians, we express our belief in this love through our willingness to help those who need us. But we must be bold and daring in our efforts to help. We must extend ourselves and take risks. We must be reckless with our love and passionate in our service, and we can be, if we remember we ourselves are loved without limit.

Epilogue

Endtime and Renewal

I have a favorite hiking trail, not far from my parents' home in Briarcliff, New York. It is a special place for me, enough removed from roads and houses so that it's possible to imagine I'm in true wilderness. There are whitetail deer and many species of birds, and squirrels in such numbers as to seem ever present. The trail is crossed by shallow streams easily waded. It's a good place to go to center oneself and think things over.

In the autumn and winter of 1996, I retreated to this trail whenever I could. There was a problem at work, a problem with me, and I knew it. It was an increasing disinterest in the administrative part of my job and all it entailed. I was happier helping in the food pantry than at staff meetings and meetings with the bishop. I was losing patience with budget problems and the demands of the Chancery. These became increasingly bothersome as I gave more attention to working personally with people in need.

I was also discouraged by the Chancery's refusal to sanction the expansion of diocesan social services into the city of Passaic. This decision, as I've already stated, was based on fiscal concerns I considered unfounded, and prevented Catholic Charities from bringing the Church's presence to a part of the diocese that would benefit from it in many ways. I had never believed I should be tentative or overly cautious about expanding services to people, but this whole episode seemed to say I would have to be so from now on.

My resignation, early in the spring of 1997, surprised almost everyone at work. I received many calls and letters of support from staff members who were kind enough to say that they appreciated what I had done and tried to do, and that I would be missed. It was painful to say good-bye and the memory of doing so is painful still. Paterson is not a city of resounding beauty or exceptional historic significance. It is beautiful and important because of those who labor and live there. The daily presence of so many good people is the loss I most regret.

In this book, I have written about sadness and suffering, but joy was present, too. Joy comes when we lose ourselves in caring for one another, when we turn away from gain and self-absorption for love's sake. This joy is genuine and always accessible. Many of the people I tried to help revealed it to me in return for meeting them.

"Coming and going, always at home"[5] is my favorite Zen saying. In six words it expresses the essence of our lives and of our relationship to God. We are never lost because from birth we are with Him. Our lives are not meaningless; what happens to us is important because He remains within us. We are His daughters and sons, heirs to His mansion, perpetually welcome to the feast prepared for us.

After fifty years of living, after nearly dying, I have finally learned to appreciate each day as a gift. I no longer worry about the future, having learned what is important about time and place: we must use what we are given, moment by moment, wherever we may be, to care for one another as Christ would have us. He asks us to love without restraint, mindful that coming or going, we are surely home.

Notes

1. Bernardin, Joseph Cardinal. *The Gift of Peace*. Chicago: Loyola Press, 1997, p. 46.

2. Merton, Thomas. "Merton's Talks to Monks: Becoming Our True Self." Tape #A2339. Kansas City, MO: The National Catholic Reporter Publishing Co., 1989. See also Schloegl, Irmgard. *The Wisdom of the Zen Masters*. New York: New Directions Books, 1976, p. 39.

3. Bode, Richard. *Beachcombing at Miramar*. New York: Warner Books, Inc., 1996, pp. 145–146.

4. Wiesel, Elie. *Four Hasidic Masters and Their Struggle against Melancholy*. Notre Dame, IN: University of Notre Dame Press, 1978, pp. 67–69.

5. Schloegl, Irmgard. *The Wisdom of the Zen Masters*. New York: New Directions Books, 1976, p. 26.